WHICH IS IT?*

lovable or loveable
ceiling or cieling
changeable or changable
forcing or forceing
dying or dieing
advisable or adviseable
judgment or judgement
noticeable or noticable
enforcing or enforceing

If you're unsure of any of these,
help is on the way.

*The first word in each pair is the correct one.

Also available in this series

GRAMMAR 101
WRITING 101

SPELLING
101

CLAUDIA SORSBY

Produced by The Philip Lief Group, Inc.

St. Martin's Paperbacks

Produced by The Philip Lief Group, Inc.

SPELLING 101

ISBN: 0-312-95974-5

Printed in the United States of America

St. Martin's Paperbacks edition/August 1996

10   9   8   7   6   5

Contents

CONTENTS

Introduction

Spelling ability has nothing to do with intelligence. It has a lot to do with developing a familiarity with words, an ability to recognize them and, equally important, a similar ability to recognize when they don't "look right."

English is considered by many to be among the most confusing languages to spell correctly. Most of the alphabet-based languages seem to be much more consistent than English in their use of letters to represent sounds. Why does English, on the other hand, have so many maddening exceptions? (Of course, things could be much worse, since character-based languages such as Chinese don't use letters to make up words and require their speakers and writers to learn thousands of characters to represent all of the words.)

The problem with English is also its greatest strength; English is one of the most flexible and absorbent languages in the world, and has evolved simultaneously with Britain's complicated history. Over the centuries, Britain was conquered by the Anglo-Saxons (who spoke a Germanic language), the Danes, and the French. Over time, all of those languages were combined by the people living in Britain into what we now recognize as English, and so we have words from all those different languages.

Moreover, English has never stopped developing. When new words are needed, some languages have trouble creating them; the French began the Académie Française specifically to regulate new words. English has no such governing body; when English speakers need new words, the terminology is either made up, or taken from somebody else. English speakers are cheerful magpies, good-natured thieves who are constantly adding to the messy nest of language. This provides us with an incredibly rich variety of words to draw upon when we want to express ourselves.

The price we pay for this diversity and depth is a language that is tougher than most to spell. English looks odd because, unlike most other languages, its words don't come from a single source. Most French words are based on Latin roots (this is why it is known as a Romance language) and follow rules of spelling based on Latin grammar. English, however, has not one source but several. There are some words that follow French rules, some that follow German, some that follow Old Norse, and . . . combine this with our unfailing readiness to create words to describe new technologies or new ideas (*microchip, computer, deconstructionism*, to name a few), and spelling quickly becomes complicated.

There have been some attempts to standardize English spelling, but none have succeeded, and it may be just as well. As it stands, our crazy English shows off its etymology, history, and connections between words. If we regularized our spelling, we'd lose all of that. Also, current English is flexible enough that it allows people with different accents and pronunciations to communicate. If we were to standardize our spelling by sound, whose accent would become the standard? Regional and class accents already cause confusion; they don't need to cause spelling mistakes, too.

This book offers you 101 rules to help you find your way through the thicket of English spelling. Of course, few of these rules are absolutes; one of the trickiest aspects of English is the enormous number of exceptions it allows (some of the rules are devoted to these exceptions). The trick is not to give up in frustration, but to understand that paying careful attention to the words you use can help you spell them better over time.

Why bother? Because spelling counts. Anyone who says otherwise is selling something. Spelling mistakes are distracting to your reader, and if they are serious or frequent enough they can actually prevent someone from understanding what you are trying to say. Even if your meaning survives, though, your credibility as a writer does not. No one knows how to spell every word, but everyone is capable of checking their work. If you hand in a memo or a report that's riddled with mistakes, it not only tells the world that you can't spell, it sends an even more serious message: that you don't care enough about either your work or your reader to check it over. This can lead to the following line of thought: "Gee, if you don't check your spelling, you probably don't check your facts either. Why should I trust you? In fact, why should I bother reading this?"

A note about spell-checkers, which will be discussed in detail in Rule 101. The thing to keep in mind about them is quite simple: Although they are recommended tools for reviewing your work, they do not replace the need for human proofreading. Do not rely solely on spell-checkers, or else your copy may end up containing typos that even a five-year-old child would detect. If you would like more information on specific problems in writing, there are two other books in this series that may be of use to you: *Writing 101*, which offers instruction on some of the finer points of writing; and *Grammar 101*, which offers instruction on the more black-and-white rules of standard English.

I strongly recommend that you invest in a good dictionary, such as *The Merriam-Webster Dictionary* (which will also be of use when performing the exercises and quizzes within this book) A good thesaurus, such as *Roget's 21st Century Thesaurus,* edited by Barbara Kipfer, is also helpful. If you have a computer with a CD-ROM drive, *The American Heritage Dictionary* provides the power of a dictionary cross-referenced with hyperlinking to a thesaurus. For guidelines on specifics for book publishing, *The Chicago Manual of Style* remains the standard.

I could not have written this book without the help of assistants Emily Fraser and Sahngmie Lah. Gary M. Krebs, my editor in New York, put up with the vicissitudes of trans-Atlantic mail while I was living and working in England. And of course, none of this would have gotten done without the constant encouragement of my husband, Daniel Hillman. Any errors, of course, are mine alone.

—CHCQS
October 1995
Cambridge, England

The Rules

1. Don't be afraid to admit what you don't know

Many people don't like to ask how to spell words because they don't want to admit that they didn't know the word in the first place. This is a common but foolhardy approach. Asking questions to avoid making mistakes is almost never a bad idea; but charging ahead blindly when you don't know what you're doing almost always is.

Recognizing that you don't know something is the first step in dealing with almost any problem. Don't be embarrassed; smile, make a joke or a self-deprecating remark, and then ask someone for a correct spelling. "Oh, I can never remember—does anyone know how many *r*s there are in 'embarrassed'?" Smart people know that it's wise to ask questions. People who are quick to pounce on other people's weaknesses are usually most concerned with hiding their own, so don't worry about them. (This is actually one of the good points about spell-checkers [see Rule 101]: They offer a sense of anonymity, since no one else can tell how much help you are getting.)

Everyone has his or her own mental blocks and blind spots when it comes to spelling. Using the rules in this book will help you find ways to approach a great many words, but if you are really stuck, don't hesitate to ask for help. Copyeditors and proofreaders get paid specifically to catch other people's spelling and grammatical mistakes, and they use dictionaries and rule books more than most people. Professionals know a lot about words, but they are also the first to admit when they don't know something, and look for further assistance when they need it.

2. Always ask people how they spell their names

There is one instance where you must always ask how to spell something, and no dictionary or computer will be of help: name spelling. When writing down a person's first name, last name, or both, always ask for it to be fully spelled out. Even the most common-sounding name can have an unusual spelling to it.

Proper names are problematic, because often there are two or more acceptable spellings and you have no way of knowing which way any given person spells his or her name. If you have correspondence from the person, or a book or list with their name in it, that's a good start, but it's always best to confirm it with the person directly. (After all, how do you know the list-compiler got it right?)

EXAMPLES: Michelle/Michele/Michel
Lyn/Lynn/Lynne/Lin
Smith/Smyth/Smythe
Jamie/Jami/Jamey
Alyson/Allyson/Allison/Alison

The same also applies to corporate names. Pay special attention to them, since in the past several years it has become fashionable to use nonstandard capitalization in company names or products.

EXAMPLE: WordPerfect is one of the most well-known culprits.

Unfortunately, this fashion is spreading to other industries as well.

EXAMPLES: Kool-Aid
           Absolut
           Quik

3. Know the differences between American spelling and British spelling

The old joke about America and England being two countries separated by a common language aside, the spelling differences that occur are not terribly difficult to handle. Few of them are drastic enough to prevent comprehension, although it is true that some differences in vocabulary can cause some embarrassment. (To mention just one: In British slang, to "knock someone up" means to knock on his or her door or call, while in American slang, it refers to making a woman pregnant.) Most of the differences simply come down to following certain rules differently.

One of the most noticeable differences is that the British end many words with *-our*, while in the States almost of all of these words end in *-or*. Common words such as *color/colour*, *honor/honour*, and *behavior/behaviour* look subtly different, but the meaning is still clear. The British also tend to spell some word endings as *-re* that Americans spell as *-er* (e.g., *specter* vs. *spectre*). Another is that the British are much more fond of doubling the letter *l* when adding suffixes than Americans (see Rule 93). Thus, the British will discuss "travelling," while Americans will discuss "traveling," but everyone is talking about the same thing. The other well-known difference is that the British end many words with *-ise* or *-yse* that Americans end with *-ize* or *-yze* (see Rule 92). The only difference between "analysing" something and "analyzing" something is whether the writer is following British or American spelling rules.

Other American/British spelling differences will be discussed under the relevant rules. The point here is that as you pay more attention to the ways words are spelled, you should be able to recognize and understand these differences, rather than perceiving them as errors. For writing geared toward American audiences, always stick with standard U.S. spellings; otherwise, you risk being labeled a pretentious writer.

SPELLCHECK

Choose the preferred American spellings in the following sentences.

The meeting will be held in the Town (Centre/Center) on Tuesday evening.

It is Bill's responsibility to (analyze/analyse) monthly sales figures.

She was so grateful for the ride home that she dubbed me "her (savior/saviour)."

The armadillo's protective skin acts as its shield of (armor/armour).

Parts and (labor/labour) are not included in the promotional sales price.

The movers would appreciate your (labeling/labelling) all these brown boxes.

4. Whenever possible, sound words out

Probably the first spelling rule you learned as a small child is this one: Sound words out. It is also probably the rule that left you feeling completely betrayed the first time you realized how many different ways the letter pattern -*ough* can sound.

Don't give up on it too quickly, though. Sounding a word out means saying it slowly, and taking it syllable by syllable; once you've spelled all of the syllables, you've spelled the word. This works in many cases, if not most, for three reasons. First is the fact that English is not completely insane. Yes, there are a great many words that are spelled oddly, and there are often different ways of writing the same sound. That said, there are still tens of thousands of common words that do follow sounds and rules. Sounding them out will help you with them.

Second is that, as you get to know the rules better, you will still need to think about when to apply them in many cases. Again, sounding words out will help you.

The third reason has nothing to do with English and everything to do with the way we generally speak. Most of us are lazy; that's why we use contractions to shorten words — for example, "that is" to "that's," or "do not" to "don't." Often, when we speak, we slur our speech. This is not to say that most people go around sounding like the town drunk, but simply a recognition of the fact that in normal speech we drop endings, we run words together, and in general have all sorts of sloppy habits. Consciously slowing down and taking the time to actually pronounce each syllable of a word is often all you'll need to spell a word correctly. It's the equivalent of re-examining the instructions to a math problem; often, a second reading gives people the information they needed to get the answer.

5. Understand the limitations of sounding words out

Part of the usefulness of any rule lies in knowing when it is applicable and when it is not, so it is important that you understand the limitations of sounding words out.

There are two main instances when sounding words out doesn't work. The first is when there are silent letters involved. The word *bomb* doesn't sound as though it has a *b* at the end, but it does. (However, you can hear the *b* in the related word *bombardment*; see Rule 18.) Many words also end in a silent final *e* (see Rule 44). The *e* is there to control the sound of another vowel, earlier in the word, but if you don't know that, you might not know that last *e* is there either. For instance, many people abbreviate their references to the Vietnam War, and talk about *'Nam*. The word *name* sounds different only because the final *e* lengthens the sound of the *a*.

The other instance in which sounding words out won't help you is when you know what the sound is, but don't know which of the multiple ways it could be spelled is correct. Take the word *enough*: The second syllable could be spelled *-nough*, *-nuff*, or just *-nuf*, since these all represent the same sound. Only the first is correct (despite the blandishments of advertisers), but how can you tell? Luckily, the next 96 rules are here to help you find out.

6. Beware of homonyms

A *homonym* is a word that sounds like another word but has a different meaning and spelling. Sometimes homonyms occur when a regular word is confused with a contraction (see Rule 98 on using apostrophes), such as the difference between *your* and *you're*. Simply remembering that homonyms exist and keeping an eye out for them is the key to avoiding much confusion and misleading language.

EXAMPLES: Here are some common homonyms with their respective definitions.

aloud: using the voice to be clearly heard
allowed: permitted

bail: prison payment
bale: a bundle of hay

cannon: artillery piece
canon: an authoritative list

cereal: wheat product
serial: relating to a series

cite: to indicate
sight: seeing ability
site: location

dual: relating to a group of two
duel: a fight between two, usually with swords or pistols

to: in a direction toward, for, concerning
too: also
two: the number

SPELLCHECK

Choose which homonym is correct.

George has a (flair/flare) for writing excellent proposals.

That was a bad (break/brake) when your computer exploded.

Gary loves ice cream for (desert/dessert), but would not (desert/dessert) his family and friends for a piece of cake.

(Your/You're) (to/too/two) tired (to/too/two) stay up late.

The music recording (session/cession) seemed to go on interminably.

7. Beware of words that are *almost* identical in pronunciation

There are also many words that are not homonyms but yet are close enough in sound to cause their own variety of spelling confusion. Some of these are well known, and some are not. When in doubt, try to think of related words, to make sure that the one you are writing is really the one you want.

EXAMPLES: affect: to influence something (verb); emotional aspect (noun)
effect: to make something happen (verb); a result (noun)

ensure: to make certain
insure: to issue insurance for

merry: jovial, festive
marry: to bind in wedlock

weather: the condition of the atmosphere
whether: if it be the case that

SPELLCHECK

Choose the correct word from the two similarly pronounced words given in parentheses.

My older sister is the legal (air, heir) to my grandfather's estate.

The legislature meets in the nation's (Capital/Capitol) building.

That high school locker room (wreaks/reeks) of smelly gym socks.

8. Understand how words are created

When tackling any aspect of the English language, it is often helpful to understand the various elements of words. Most words begin with a *root* or *main* word, which contains the basic core of meaning. Other pieces may be tacked on to change or amplify the meaning in some way, but the core of the word will tell you what it's about. Take the verb *to walk*, which means to move by the action of one's legs. If you added *-ed* to the end of that main word, you have created the past tense of the verb, *walked*. This means that someone performed the action of walking, at some time in the past. There are many words involving *walk*, such as **walk**about, **walk**-on, and **walk**up, but they all have that root word in there somewhere, and that tells the reader something about that word. The root explains something about the meaning of the word and also something about how at least part of the word is spelled.

Words can be changed in two ways: by the addition of *prefixes* or *suffixes*. A prefix is a phrase or syllable that is attached to the front of the word, while a suffix is attached to the end of the word (in the previous example, the *-ed* stuck onto the end of *walk* is a suffix). Sometimes, more than one prefix or suffix can be tacked on (as in the word re + visit + ed = revisited).

The useful thing about prefixes and suffixes is that they often carry meanings of their own. Put that together with the root word, and you can often tell both what the word means, and how to spell it. For example, the prefix *pre-* means "before," or "in front of" (from the Latin). *Fix* means "to place" or "fasten se-

curely." So, even if you didn't know what a prefix
was, you could figure it out by taking it apart into its
component parts. Since you know how the prefix *pre-*
is spelled, you'd have a good shot at spelling it right,
even if you'd only heard it.

Here is a list of common word elements (prefixes,
suffixes, and roots), together with their meanings.

Word Element	Definition	Examples
aer(o)	air, aircraft	aerial, aerobics, aerodrome
agr(o)	farming, fields	agriculture, agrarian
ambi	both	ambidextrous, ambivalent
ante	before	antechamber, antenatal
anthrop(o)	man, mankind	misanthrope, philanthropy
anti	against	antifreeze, antiwar
aqua	water	aquarium, aquatic
arch(ae)(o)	old	archaic, archeology
aud	hearing	audible, audiotape
auto	self	automat, autobiography
bi	two	bicycle, biped, bimonthly
biblio	book	bibliography, bibliophile
bio	life	biography, biology
carn	flesh	carnal, carnivore
cent	one hundred	centipede, century

chron(o)	time	chronic, chronological
cid(e)	kill, killer	homicidal, patricide
cracy/crat	rule, ruler	democracy, democrat
dexter	right	dexterity, dextrous
dis	not	disrespect, dissatisfaction
dys	difficult, bad	dysfunction, dyspepsia
equ(a)(i)	equality	equable, equilateral
ex	out of	excise, expel, export
fore	before	forearm, forewarn
geo	Earth	geography, geology
gram/graph(y)	write	autograph, graphology, telegram
gyn(o)	woman	gynecology, misogynist
heter(o)	other, different	heterogeneous, heterosexual
homo	same	homogeneous, homosexual
hydr(o)	water	hydrant, dehydrated, hydrofoil
hyper	above, beyond	hyperactive, hypertext
in	not	inanimate, invisible
inter	between	international, interstate

logy	study of	archeology, musicology
micro	small	microscope, micrometer
mis	error, failure	misconduct, misfire, misread
mono	single, one	monoculture, monogamous
naut	sailing, sailor	astronaut, nautical
omni	all	omniscient, omnipotent
ped(o)	child	pediatrician
phil(e)	love	philanthropy, philosophy
phob(e)(ic)	fear, hate	claustrophobia, Francophobe
phon(e)	sound	phonetic, telephone
pre	before, in front	precede, predict, preheat
pro	favor, forward	proclaim, progress, prorevolutionary
pseudo	false	pseudo-intellectual
re	again or back	redo, remind, return
retro	backwards	retroactive, retrograde
rupt	break	disruptive, rupture
sci	know	conscientious, science
scope	see, view	telescope, "scope out" (slang)

sub	under	subdue, submarine, submit
super	above	superintendent, superior, superman
tele	far	telegraph, television
trans	across	translate, transmit, transparent
un	not, reverse	uneven, unmade, unusual
vis	see	visible, visit, vista
vor	eat	omnivorous, voracious

SPELLCHECK

Try to define the following words based on the prefix definitions above. Then ask a friend to test you on spelling the ten words.

1. homogeneous
2. dyslexia
3. pseudonym
4. interrupt
5. pediatrician
6. television
7. centennial
8. ambidextrous
9. chronological
10. autobiography

9. Keep the meaning of the word in mind

The meaning of a word can often tell you a great deal about the word itself, including how it should be spelled. This is one of the strengths of our otherwise maddening spelling system.

Let's say you want to use a word meaning "someone who eats meat," and you know that there is such a word, but you're not sure how it's spelled. You know that *-vor* is the general ending for "eating," and you know that *carn* is the root for flesh or meat. Putting the two together gives you the word *carnivore*.

There's another way that keeping meaning in mind can help you, and that's with silent letters. Since related words will share roots or elements, you can think of words that are connected to the word you want, to make sure there aren't any letters you might be missing (see Rule 5). For example, many people get confused about the spelling of the word *medicine*, because they can't remember what the middle vowel is, and sounding it out isn't much help. Think of the word *medical*, though, or *medicinal*, and that will help you recognize that pesky middle vowel: *i*.

SPELLCHECK

Define the following words, but this time, come up with at least one other related word for each. (Or, go wild: Find as many related words as you can.) Then get someone else to test you on spelling the original words.

1. bombast
2. inflammatory

3. serendipity
4. thermos
5. judicial
6. reconcile
7. elephantine
8. penalty
9. legitimate
10. auditorium

10. Learn to recognize letter patterns

When you learn to recognize patterns of letters, it will help you develop a feel for good spelling. Many good spellers don't know any spelling rules, but they do know when a word "looks right." Part of the way they do this is by recognizing the characteristic letter patterns of their language.

One common set of letters in English is *-ough* (*brought, cough, tough*).

In French, *-être* is a common letter pattern, but it doesn't occur in English. Another common French pattern is *-eau*, and this does occur in English—in words that we've taken from French (see Rule 59).

EXAMPLES: Here are some common English-language letter patterns and a few instances of words that contain them.

-ight	right, flight
-eigh	weigh, height, sleigh
-tion	ration, function, explanation
-sion	extension, obsession
-ounce	announce, pounce, pronounce
-eau	beauty, chateau

Part of understanding letter patterns is knowing which patterns relate to which sounds. Many people know many more words by sound than they do by eye. Given that there are some very good reasons why English includes some of the more unusual letter patterns that it does, it behooves spellers to know what they are. (For one thing, if you can't spell the

beginning of a word—or at least come close—you
won't be able to find it in a dictionary.)

SPELLCHECK

*Come up with at least six inadmissable letter patterns
for English (for example, triple letters, such as teeem-
ing).*

11. Recognize all the possible spellings for the vowel *a* and its sound

Fortunately, English has limits to its insanity. Yes, there are often several ways to represent any given sound, but there is not an infinite number — usually, it doesn't even get to double digits. The short *a* sound, for example, can be written in only eight different ways.

EXAMPLES: a — as in c**a**t
au — as in l**au**ghter
al — as in s**al**ve
ea — as in b**ea**r
e — as in s**e**rgeant
aa — as in baz**aa**r
ai — as in pl**ai**d
i — as in mer**i**ngue

The long *a* sound offers even more possibilities. You will notice that some of the patterns appear in both places, of course, just to make life more interesting.

EXAMPLES: ay — as in p**ay**
ai — as in p**ai**d
a + consonant + e — as in n**a**m**e**
ea — as in br**ea**k
au — as in g**au**ge
ei — as in n**ei**gh
ey — as in ob**ey**

24

é—résumé (from French)
ae—Gaelic

SPELLCHECK

Choose the correct spelling for the various a *sounds in the following sentences.*

I wonder how that (sleigh/slay) will hold nine people.

Put the baby into his (cradle/creighdle).

Bell bottoms are simply a passing (fad/fade).

The (pain/payne) of the surgery has subsided.

12. Recognize all the possible spellings for the vowel *e* and its sound

E is said to be the letter most commonly used in the English language. Most Scrabble or Boggle players find this out the moment they hit a round that lacks this crucial letter. Unsurprisingly, there are quite a few ways to spell its sound. There are nine ways to represent the short *e* sound, and an even dozen ways to represent the long *e* sound.

First, the short *e*.

EXAMPLES: e—as in p**e**t
ea—as in br**ea**d
ai—as in s**ai**d
ay—as in s**ay**s
a—as in m**a**ny
eo—as in l**eo**pard
ei—as in h**ei**fer
ie—as in fr**ie**nd
ae—as in **ae**sthetic

Next, the long *e*.

EXAMPLES: ee—as in b**ee**r
ea—as in p**ea**l
e + consonant + e—as in sc**ene**
e—as in **e**vangelical
ie—as in f**ie**ld
ei—as in w**ei**rd
ey—as in donk**ey**
eo—as in p**eo**ple

oe—as in ph**oe**nix
i—as in pol**i**ce
ay—as in qu**ay**
ae—as in C**ae**sar

SPELLCHECK

Choose the correct spelling for the various e sounds in the following sentences.

These pencils do not contain real (lead/led).

(Pleese/Please) do not smoke.

All entrepreneurs want to increase their personal (welth/wealth).

My favorite place in France is the beautiful city of (Nice/Niece).

13. Recognize all the possible spellings for the vowel *i* and its sound

The vowel *i* has two main sounds, its short version and its long version. It is one of the less complicated vowel sounds to spell. Here are the spelling possibilities for the short version.

EXAMPLES: i—as in **pit**
y—as in **hymn**
ie—as in **sieve**
ei—as in for**eig**n
ai—as in mount**ai**n
o—as in w**o**men
u—as in b**u**siness
e—as in **E**nglish

Here are the ways to spell the long version (notice that there are fewer).

EXAMPLES: i—as in **isle**
ai—as in **aisle**
ie—as in p**ie**
i + consonant + e—as in **ice**
igh—as in l**igh**t
eigh—as in h**eigh**t
ei—**ei**derdown
y—as in tr**y**

Note that the word *try* has a long *i* sound because the *y* ends the word. Typically, the letter *y* in a word would still require an *i* next to it for it to maintain that sound (as in *trying*). The *try* combination of letters more often than not has a short *y* sound (as in *tryst*), whereas the *try* combination either has a long *i* sound (as in *trial*) or short (as in *trip*).

SPELLCHECK

Choose the correct spelling for the various i *sounds in the following sentences.*

His right (I/eye) is swollen from the fight.

The drinking (fountin/fountain) is spouting brown water.

The team was finally (triumphant/tryumphant) against its main rival.

I wish you would stop (wyning/whining)!

14. Recognize all the possible spellings for the vowel *o* and its sound

As any singer knows, vowel sounds can get complicated. The letter *o* has two different sorts of sounds; the first pair will be covered here, and the next set in the following rule (see Rule 15).

First, there's the regular short *o* sound. This isn't too bad, actually, since there are only five different ways to spell it.

EXAMPLES: o—as in p**o**t
ou—as in c**ou**gh
a—as in w**a**tch
au—as in c**au**ght
aw—as in s**aw**

Then, there's the long *o*. There are twelve ways to represent this sound.

EXAMPLES: o—as in **o**pen
o + consonant + e—as in s**o**l**e**
oa—as in s**oa**p
oe—as in t**oe**
oo—as in fl**oo**r
ou—as in s**ou**l
ow—as in gr**ow**
ew—as in s**ew**
ol—as in f**ol**k
eau—as in bur**eau** (from French)

au—as in m**au**ve
eo—as in y**eo**man

SPELLCHECK

Choose the correct spelling for the various o sounds in the following sentences.

You reap what you (sough/sow).

Tim always does a (thorough/thorow) job cleaning the kitchen after dinner.

The kitten (cot/caught/cawt) an eye infection from its mother.

Since when do you (mone/moan) in your sleep?

15. Recognize all the possible spellings for the sounds *aw, ow,* and *oi*

There are three other major sounds that are based on the letter *o* (see Rule 14 for the first ones). The first is the *aw* sound.

EXAMPLES: aw—as in s**aw**
au—as in c**au**ght
o—as in t**o**rtoise
oa—as in b**oa**r
ou—as in **ou**ght

Second is the *ow* sound (immortalized by the character of Eliza Doolittle in the musical *My Fair Lady*, as well as anyone who's ever hammered his or her thumb).

EXAMPLES: ow—as in n**ow**
ou—as in **ou**t
au—as in s**au**erkraut

Finally we have the *oi* sound, which can only be spelled in two ways.

EXAMPLES: oy—as in b**oy**
oi—as in p**oi**son

SPELLCHECK

Choose the correct spelling for the various aw, ow, and oi sounds in the following sentences.

Farmer Joe will finish (plowing/ploughing)* his field any day now, I reckon.

I (taught/tawt) my sister how to play the tuba.

Amy started (boyling/boiling) water for tea.

*The correct choice in this example is either or both of the spellings given. Although the former is more common than the latter, both are acceptable.

16. Recognize all the possible spellings for the vowel *u* and its sound

The vowel *u* has two main sounds, the long and the short. There are quite a few ways to spell the long version, but only five letter combinations represent the short version. Here they are.

EXAMPLES: u—as in c**u**t
oo—as in bl**oo**d
ou—as in d**ou**ble
o—as in s**o**n
a—as in w**a**s

There are even more ways of representing the long *u*.

EXAMPLES: oo—as in b**oo**t
u—as in tr**u**th
ue—as in gl**ue**
o + consonant + e—as in m**o**v**e**
oe—as in sh**oe**
eu—as in rh**eu**matism
ui—as in fr**ui**t
ou—as in thr**ou**gh

SPELLCHECK

Choose the correct spelling for the various u-sounds in the following sentences.

That tantrum put him in (dubble/double) (trubble/trouble) with his older brother.

(Hoo/Who) (could/cood) possibly have done that much damage?

The (flough/flu) has been vicious this winter.

17. Recognize all the possible spellings for the sound *yoo*

This is a rather strange sound, since it seems to be a combination of the letters *y* and *o*, but they don't appear in spelling it. Since *y* can count as either a vowel or a consonant, this can be interpreted as its vowel sound (see Rule 32). There are some words where it can be particularly tricky, especially in the word *ewe*. Luckily, there are only five ways of representing it.

EXAMPLES: ew — as in **ewe**, **few**
u — as in **use**
ue — as in c**ue**
eu — as in f**eu**d
eau — as in b**eau**ty

SPELLCHECK

Correctly spell the misspelled words in italics.

They were arrested for attempting to steal a *pyew* from church property.

That film was a bit *groosome* toward the end.

A *pewny* mouse darted across the hallway.

Steve ate more than a *fue* of the snacks.

My *myoosic* skills would be better if I weren't tone deaf.

18. Recognize all the possible spellings for the sound *b* and that a *b* can be silent

Consonants are generally easier sounds to represent than vowels. Some combination sounds can be spelled in several ways, but overall consonants present fewer chances for the ear to betray the eye (this may also explain why irregularities seem somehow harder when they occur with consonants). The sound of the letter *b*, for example, can only be spelled in two ways.

EXAMPLES:　b—as in **b**ook
　　　　　　bb—as in bu**bb**ly

Since *bb* can never start a word, knowing this rule can make it much easier to find words in dictionaries, when necessary.

There is one tricky thing about the consonant *b*, however. Silent *b*s lurk in seemingly misleading places, such as in the middle and at the end of words that don't contain a *b* sound.

EXAMPLES:　dum**b**
　　　　　　thum**b**
　　　　　　bom**b**ing
　　　　　　plum**b**er

Be familiar with these silent *b*s; see Rule 24 for more information on silent consonants.

SPELLCHECK

Correctly spell the misspelled words in italics.

The teacher was *bombbarded* with questions about last week's lesson.

Wipe the *drible* off the baby's face.

She wants to avoid the briars and *brambbles* of the meadow.

19. Recognize all the possible spellings for the sound *d*

There are only four ways of representing the sound of the letter *d* (and one of them requires the help of a vowel).

EXAMPLES: d—as in **deed**
           dd—as in te**dd**y
           ed—as in wall**ed**
           ld—as in cou**ld**

The real confusion comes when people slur their speech enough to mix up a *d* sound with a *t* sound. There are some scientific, linguistic reasons why we often do so, but it still wreaks havoc on spelling. Careful enunciation is the only way to stay out of that little (not "liddle") trap.

EXAMPLES: Here are some words that may look right as spelled in the first column (followed by the proper spellings in the second column):

Incorrect	Correct
kindergarden	kindergarten
lieutendant	lieutenant
polluded	polluted

SPELLCHECK

Choose the correct spelling in the following sentences.

The (thermometer/thermomeder) reads 85 degrees.

Our (floodded/flooded) basement is the neighborhood attraction.

Frank did not appreciate it when Joan gave him an (ultimatum/ultimadum).

(Wood/Would) you please come here?

20. Recognize all the possible spellings for the sound *f*

F was one of the sounds that George Bernard Shaw famously made fun of, when he complained that English spelling was so illogical that the word *fish* could just as easily be spelled "ghoti" if one applied certain rules in the wrong circumstances: *gh* as in lau*gh*; *o* as in w*o*men; and *ti* as in mo*ti*on. While it is true that *-gh* is one of the ways of spelling the sound of the letter *f*, Shaw was exaggerating a bit. (For starters, *gh* never sounds like *f* when used at the beginning of a word.)

EXAMPLES: f—as in **f**i**f**e
ff—as in o**ff**
ph—as in **ph**ony
gh—as in cou**gh**
lf—as in ha**lf**
ft—as in so**ft**en

The *f* sound does not vary greatly in its pronunciation; almost always, an *f* at the beginning of a word has the same sound as an *f* or an *ff* in the middle of a word. For example: fudge, coffee, classify. At the end of a word, *ff* will usually have a soft sound, as in o**ff**. When there is a single *f* at the end of a word, like of, it tends to be pronounced more like a *v*. Being familiar with these pronunciation rules makes it easier to spell words containing the letter *f*.

The letter *f* has a special property: it often becomes *ve* when made plural, as in *half* and *halves*. See Rule 56 for more information on pluralizing *f*s. Also, for further distinctions of the *f* sounds, see Rules 39 and 40.

SPELLCHECK

Choose the correct spelling in the following sentences.

The (gruff/grough) professor made a rude (reference/refference) to my tardiness.

I wish the entire (staf/staff) a good holiday.

Jim's dream apartment is a (loft/loff) in Soho.

Get (off/of) (off/of) my foot!

That big hog has been glaring at those three little (wolfs/wolves) all day.

21. Recognize all the possible spellings for the sound *g* and the silent *g*

The hard *g* sound can be represented in English in one of five ways. It would have been four, but the first English printer, William Caxton, had spent many years abroad and liked to insert an *h* after many *g*s. (This was in the days before dictionaries, so no one could tell him he was wrong.)

EXAMPLES: g—as in **gag**
gg—as in gi**gg**le
gh—as in **gh**ost
gu—as in **gu**ard
x—e**x**ample

Note that the letter *x* (as in *example*, above) is really a combination of the sound *gz*. However, the *x* can also have a *ks* sound (as in the final syllable of Xer*ox*; see Rule 23).

The real problem with the letter *g* is that it can often appear silently in a word, lurking with no apparent purpose other than to trip up unwary spellers (see Rules 20 and 39 to avoid this).

See Rule 22 for words spelled with a *g* pronounced as a *j*, like usage.

SPELLCHECK

Find the hard g sounds in the following sentences.

Dill gherkins are my favorite types of pickles.

Chemistry students must wear goggles in the lab.

Try not to mispronounce the word recognize.

22. Recognize all the possible spellings for the sound *j*

Sometimes confusion arises here, between the sound of a soft *g* and the normal sound of a *j*. Often a *gg* will sound like a hard *g* (*aggregate*), and in other instances (such as with *exaggerate*) it will be a pure *j* sound. Do not allow yourself to be fooled by such seeming inconsistencies. The important thing is to recognize all of the eight different possibilities, which are listed below, and your visual senses will take over from there.

EXAMPLES: j—as in **j**udge
dg—as in ju**dg**ment
dge—as in e**dge**
g—as in **g**em
ge—as in a**ge**
gg—as in exa**gg**erate
dj—a**dj**ust
d—gra**d**uate

SPELLCHECK

Find the soft g or pure j sounds in the following sentences.

One's gender is determined by one's genes.

The gel you use in your hair is causing it to look greasy and grimy.

Please adjust your chair so that it is not near the edge of the cliff.

23. Recognize all the possible spellings for the sound *k* and the silent *k*

The sound *k* has the most possible letter combinations and the greatest number of phonetic representations. Take a look at the list below to see how many different ways the *k* sound can be written.

EXAMPLES: k—as in **k**ey
c—as in **c**on
ck—as in sti**ck**
cc—as in a**cc**ount
qu—as in opa**qu**e
ch—as in **ch**aotic
cqu—as in a**cqu**ire
cch—as in sa**cch**arine
ch—as in **sch**ism
lk—as in wa**lk**
kh—as in **kh**aki
x—as in e**x**tra [ks]; as in lu**x**ury [ksh]

The letter *k* also appears quite frequently in words that don't have a *k* sound at all. In these cases, the *k* precedes another consonant and the word is pronounced with the sound of the second consonant (which is usually an *n*).

EXAMPLES: know
knife
knight
kneel

See Rule 25 for more information on the silent *k*.

SPELLCHECK

Correct the misspelled words in italics in the following sentences.

Sailors *kneed* to *no* how to tie several intricate *nots*.

These files are absolutely *kaotic*.

My aunt hand-stitched a *kwilt* for her young niece.

Draw me two *obleak* lines.

24. Recognize all the possible spellings for the sound *m* and watch out for silent letters

M is a sound that causes many problems because it is frequently combined with other letters that remain sneakily silent. Don't panic, and don't go into fits trying to pronounce *phlegm*, either: Look at the following list of ways to represent the sound *m*.

EXAMPLES: m—as in **mo**m
mm—as in com**m**on
mn—as in sole**mn**
mb—as in bo**mb**
lm—as in ca**lm**
gm—as in paradi**gm**
chm—as in dra**chm**
nm—as in gover**nm**ent

Many of the words that involve these silent letters are good examples of how related words can help you spell the one you want. *Phlegm* is pretty tricky, but remembering *phlegmatic* can help, since the silent *g* becomes a hard *g* sound. You might leave the final *-n* off *solemn*, but not if you think of *solemnity* first.

SPELLCHECK

Choose the correct spelling in the following sentences.

I love the white (columns/colums) on that old house.

Singing a (hymm/hymn) at the end of the sermon is common in the Protestant church.

Florida's (palm/pomn) trees lure vacationers from all over the country.

25. Recognize all the possible spellings for the sound *n*

There are only half a dozen ways to spell the sound *n*, but they cause far more than their share of spelling trouble. This is because several of them have silent letters that tend to appear at the beginning of words. This makes them both difficult to spell, *and* difficult to look up: a double whammy. The silent *k* and the silent *g* have both been previously discussed (see Rules 23 and 21, respectively).

EXAMPLES: n — as in **n**o
nn — as in su**nn**y
kn — as in **kn**it
gn — as in **gn**arl
pn — as in **pn**eumonia
mn — as in **mn**emonic

Other than being familiar with such oddities of the English language, there is no infallible way to remember silent *k*s, *g*s, and *p*s or to distinguish among variances in silent letters that form *n* (*kn* and *gn*). But, luckily, if you can't seem to understand why some words are spelled with a single *n* and others are spelled with *nn*, you can think about the pronunciations. More often than not, *n* following a vowel makes the vowel sound long (as in po**n**y or di**n**e). With *nn*, the vowel sound is shorter, as in fu**nn**y and fa**nn**ing.

SPELLCHECK

Choose the correct spelling in the following sentences.

The roots of the old oak tree were tangled and (knarled/narled/gnarled) with the elm's roots.

Tom will sharpen his (knife/nife/gnife) for the trip.

Jerry is a very (funy/funny) guy.

Remember to turn left at the stop (sine/sign).

26. Recognize all the possible spellings for the sound *p*

P could be a very nice letter for spellers, since there are only three ways of representing its sound. Unhappily, one of those ways involves another one of those pesky silent letters. Moreover, *p* itself is one of the letters that tends to be silent (and mess up others; see Rules 25 and 40).

EXAMPLES: p—as in **p**o**p**
pp—ha**pp**y
ph—she**ph**erd

To understand why some words are spelled with a single *p* and others are spelled with *pp*, think about the pronunciations. Usually, *p* following a vowel makes the vowel sound long (as in Po**p**e or gra**p**e). With a *pp*, the vowel sound is shorter, as in di**pp**ing and ha**pp**ening.

*P*s are used in other words, such as tele**p**hone and **p**neumonia, but remember that *ph* may have an *f* sound and that *p* may be silent before some consonants, as in the example **p**neumonia. The reason the *ph* combination in words like she**ph**erd has a distinguishable *p* sound is the syllabication: shep'herd. See Rule 40 for more information on the *f* sound of *ph*, and Rule 25 for more on silent letters before *n*.

SPELLCHECK

Choose the correct spelling in the following sentences.

Peter (Pipper/Piper) picked pickled (peppers/pepers).

He is changing the (appearance/apearance) of his dorm room.

Autumn is a good time for picking (aples/apples).

27. Recognize all the possible spelling for the sound *r*

The nice thing about all the representations of the sound *r* is that all of them do indeed include the letter *r*. (As the other rules show, this is not at all to be assumed). Another nice thing is that there are only five of them altogether.

EXAMPLES: r—as in **r**oa**r**
           rr—as in fu**rr**y
           wr—as in **wr**y
           rh—as in **rh**yme
           rrh—as in dia**rrh**ea

The problem again is that several of these possible spellings can occur at the beginning of a word, making it tougher to find the word in reference works. Keep the above spellings firmly in mind to avoid such problems.

Note that a word can begin with an *r* or *wr* to make the *r* sound (*ring* meaning the sound of a phone or *wring* to mean compress or squeeze). See Rule 31 for more information on the silent *w*.

SPELLCHECK

Correct the misspelled words in italics in the following sentences.

Sam is an all-state *restler*.

He claims that he can *reck* anything with one punch.

Harold loves to be *terified* by *horrorr* movies.

Why are you always in such a *hurrry*?

28. Recognize all the possible spellings for the sound *s*

S is another one of those pesky sounds that can be represented in several different ways. Some involve silent letters, while others require the doubling of consonants. In the case of the letter *c*, matters can become truly confusing because it only takes the *s* sound in front of certain vowels: *e* (*cent*), *i* (*cite*), and *y* (*cyborg*). Vowels such as *a* (*cab*), *o* (*cover*), and *u* (*cube*) take the hard *c* sound only. Other hidden traps are noted below.

EXAMPLES: s — as in **s**ell
ss — as in pu**ss**ycat
ci — as in **ci**ty
ce — as in **ce**rtified
cy — as in **cy**st
sc — as in **sc**ent
ps — as in **ps**ychology
st — as in fa**st**en
sw — as in **sw**ord

There are only four times that the letter *c* is pronounced *s*: in the letter combinations *ce*, *ci*, *sc*, and *cy* (as in **ce**real, **ci**ty, **sc**ene, and **cy**berspace). Remember these instances to help you conquer some of the many *s*-sounding words.

SPELLCHECK

Choose the correct spelling(s) in the following sentences.

Somebody has taken my (sissors/scissors).

Helga (crossed/crosed) the street during the Don't Walk signal.

I will devise a more efficient (mesaging/messaging) (sysstem/system).

You don't need (mussle/muscle) to do well in (school/shool).

29. Recognize all the possible spellings for the sound *t*

The letter *t* by itself doesn't cause all that many difficulties. It's when other letters are added that spelling becomes confusing, especially since many of these additions are silent. With non-silent letters, the pronunciations change to varying degrees; often, as noted below with the *th* combination, the *t* takes on a new sound entirely with another letter attached. The general combinations are noted below.

EXAMPLES: t — as in **t**at
tt — as in ba**tt**le
th — as in **Th**omas
pt — as in **pt**erodactyl (or recei**pt**, at the end of a word)
bt — as in dou**bt**
ct — as in indi**ct**
ght — as in li**ght**

Luckily, there are not many cases in which *th* is pronounced *t*; it usually takes on the traditional *th* (as in **th**e or **th**ing) sound. One exception, in addition to **Th**omas, is **Th**ailand. For the most part, proper nouns aside, you can assume that there is no *th* involved in a hard *t* sound. See Rule 38 for more on the sound *th*.

As for the strange-looking combination *ght*, know that this is a commonly used English language pattern, and that it almost always carries the vowel sound that precedes it, sliding right into the *t* as in cau**ght**, mi**ght**, or hei**ght**. See Rule 10 for additional letter patterns.

To understand why some words are spelled with a

single *t* and others are spelled with *tt*, think about the pronunciations. Usually, *t* following a vowel makes the vowel sound long (as in fate or smite). With a *tt*, the vowel sound is shorter, as in witty and putty. See Rules 25 and 26 for more information about consonants that affect the vowels preceding them, and Rules 18 and 39 for silent consonants.

SPELLCHECK

Correct the misspelled words in italics in the following sentences.

I *cott* a cold while skiing last week.

She asked the cashier for a *receet* for the recipe book she purchased.

Carol has been *biten* by the MacDonalds' pig.

Bridal gowns are usually *whight* or off-*whitte*.

30. Recognize all the possible spellings for the sound *v*

The sound of the letter *v* is relatively uncomplicated when it comes to spelling. There are five ways of representing it; the only trouble arises from the fact that the letter itself only appears in three of its representations.

EXAMPLES: v—as in **v**anity
                  vv—as in sa**vv**y
                  ve—as in val**ve**
                  f—as in o**f**
                  ph—as in Ste**ph**en

If you have any difficulty with this rule, remember that many men named Stephen prefer being called Steve (although Stephe is practically never used).

The most common spellings of the *v* sound are simply the letter *v* itself, and this should be easy to remember providing your enunciation is clear. Also, you should remember that some plural *f*s become *ves*, as in knife/kni**ves** and leaf/lea**ves**. See Rule 56 for additional information on this.

SPELLCHECK

Choose the correct spelling in the following sentences.

(Velvvet/Velvet) and satin are some of the most luxurious materials available.

Dorothy has an unnatural fear of (wolffs/wolves).

Chocolate is the best (flavvor/flavor) in existence.

31. Recognize all the possible spellings for the sound *w* and the silent *w*

There are only four ways of representing the sound *w*. Two of them are fairly obvious, but the others are less so. Try saying the following examples, to make sure you get them down.

EXAMPLES: w—as in **w**ith
wh—as in **wh**en
u—as in q**u**iet
o—as in **o**ne

W is one of the consonants that can lurk silently before certain other consonants, usually *rs*. In most cases, one can visually recognize the absence of a silent *w* (*restle* looks incorrect, compared to *wrestle*). The trouble typically arises in the case of homonyms, words that sound the same but are spelled differently and have different meanings. For example, the word *wring* is correct as is, but only if you mean to indicate you are squeezing a wet towel; if you mean to indicate the sound of a doorbell, you would require the homonym *ring*. See the list below for additional silent *w*s.

EXAMPLES: **wr**ench
wrist
write

For more on silent consonants, see Rules 18, 23, and 24. See also Rule 27 for additional information on the *r* sound.

SPELLCHECK

Correct the misspelled words in italics in the following sentences.

Let's go *hole whog* with this Halloween theme.

All students are *reckwired* to know who is president.

Why not *wet* your appetite with a beverage?

The answer to the question was *rong*.

32. Recognize all the possible spellings for the sound y

The sound of the letter y in and of itself is represented in only a few ways (see Rule 17 for a combination version). A couple of them may be somewhat unexpected.

EXAMPLES: y—as in **ye**s
                i—as in op**i**nion
                j—as in hallelu**j**ah
                u—as in p**u**trid
               ew—as in **ew**e

The letter *j* sounds like *y* only in extremely rare cases. This deviant spelling should not be a big concern as you master English spelling. Usually, words ending in *y* have the *e* sound (like hard**ly**), words beginning in *y* are generally pronounced the way they look (like **y**ellow).

The word **ewe** is notable for two reasons: first, because it is pronounced with a *y* sound without containing a *y*, and second, because it is the only word beginning with the letter *e* that is pronounced like *y*.

SPELLCHECK

Choose the correct spellings in the following sentences.

I love mushrooms and (onions/onyons).

A (fugue/fyooge) is a musical piece in which the melody is constantly repeated.

(Halleluyah/Hallelujah)! There's no school today!

33. Recognize all the possible spellings for the sound z

Although the letter z is used relatively rarely in spelling, its sound is more common. There are five different ways of representing it, in fact.

EXAMPLES: z — as in **z**ebra (or si**z**e)
zz — as in fu**zz**y
ss — as in sci**ss**ors
s — as in wa**s**
x — as in **x**ylophone

Note that the letter x as in example is really a combination of the sounds gz. For more information on this sound, which does incorporate one of the many z sounds, see Rule 21.

Also be aware that many words with the letter s are pronounced with a z sound. If you remember that not too many words actually contain a z, you will be better equipped to spell z-sounding words.

SPELLCHECK

Correct the misspelled words in italics in the following sentences.

Chris put a *mussle* on the horse as she harnessed it for competition.

The filet mignon is an *eckscellent* choice.

Your wit is *razzor*-sharp.

34. Recognize all the possible spellings for the sounds *h* and *l*

These two letters, *h* and *l*, are combined in this Rule, since there are only two ways of representing either of them. First, the sound *h*.

EXAMPLES: h—as in **h**at
wh—as in **wh**o

The letter *h* at the beginning of a word is never followed by a consonant, except *y* (which passes on occasion as a vowel anyway).

EXAMPLES: **hy**drate
hybrid

The letter combination *wh* is only pronounced as *h* when it is followed by *o*, as in *whole*. But note that this is not a rule, just a potential case. Words such as *whoop* combine the *wh* sound for the same combination as in *when*.

Next, the sound of the letter *l*.

EXAMPLES: l—as in **l**id (or need**l**e)
ll—as in we**ll**

The *ll* combination is almost always found at the end or in the middle of a word. Only in a few exceptions, such as with **ll**ama and **Ll**oyd, are the two *l*s put together at the beginning of a word. Remember that it is highly irregular to see this spelling.

As you might expect, *ll* at the end of a word is pronounced with a slightly longer emphasis than *l*, as in **fall** versus **single**. This may help you spell some *l* words phonetically.

SPELLCHECK

Choose the correct spelling in the following sentences.

(Hoo/Who) is responsible for this delay?

She ought to (mingell/mingle) with more people at these parties.

Who are you going to (call/cal) about that problem?

One needs a license to (sell/sel) goods on the street.

John (folowed/followed) his instincts and wrote the letter.

Martha suffered from (hooping/whooping) cough.

35. Recognize all the possible spellings for the sound *ch*

Now that the letters of the alphabet have been taken care of, it is important to look at how certain combination sounds are represented. The first is the *ch* sound. There are five ways of spelling it.

EXAMPLES: ch—as in **ch**unk
                tch—as in ma**tch**
                t—as in fu**t**ure
                c—as in **c**ello
                cz—as in the **Cz**ech Republic

Ch is one of the English language's special compound consonants, along with many others such as *sh*, *th*, and *gh* (see Rules 37, 38, and 39 for more on these). You must recognize *ch* as a letter combination that takes on a specific pronunciation.

The combination *utu* (as in the example above, **fut**ure) takes on a *ch* sound simply because few make the effort to enunciate clearly enough to separate the *t* from the *u*. Therefore, it becomes a more easily pronounced *ch*.

SPELLCHECK

Choose the correct spellings in the following sentence.

The doctor (stitched/stiched) the (patient/pashient) up with five neat (suchures/sutures).

36. Recognize all the possible spellings for the sound *ng*

Another common combination sound is that of *-ng*. This is represented in three ways, all of which have the letter *n* in them somewhere. This sound never begins a word, but always comes either in the middle or at the end of one.

EXAMPLES: ng—as in si**ng**ing
ngue—as in to**ngue**
n—as in pla**n**k

Many people are tempted to pronounce *handkerchief* with an *ng* sound in the middle of the word. However, strictly speaking, this pronunciation is incorrect. It helps you to see the syllable markings of the word when trying to pronounce it correctly: hand'ker'chief. Speakers who are not careful about this are subject to being misinterpreted.

SPELLCHECK

Identify the three ng *sounds in the following sentence.*

After dwelling among the village people for a few days, Sir Winchester counted his blessings.

37. Recognize all the possible spellings for the sounds *sh* and *zh*

Many people get these two sounds confused, but they shouldn't. One hint is that there are many ways of representing the *sh* sound, but fewer ways of spelling the *zh* sound so, when in doubt, go with the odds. Here are the spellings for *sh*.

EXAMPLES: sh—as in **sh**eep (or fi**sh**)
ch—as in **ch**ivalrous
s—as in **s**ure
ss—as in mi**ss**ion
sc—as in con**sc**ience
c—as in o**c**ean
sch—as in **sch**illing
t—as in atten**t**ion

Now, by contrast, there are only three ways to spell the *zh* sound.

EXAMPLES: s—as in unu**s**ual
z—as in sei**z**ure
ge—as in rou**ge**

Sh is another of the English language's special compound consonants. You must recognize *sh* and its various spellings as a letter combination that takes on a specific pronunciation.

One small detail that may confuse things: Sometimes, but not often, *ss* can be pronounced *zh* instead of *sh*. The word fi**ss**ure is a good example. Also, don't forget that *ss* is usually pronounced *s*. See Rule 28 for more information on the *s* sound.

SPELLCHECK

Choose the correct spellings in the following sentences.

Susan is concerned with issues of (malnutrishion/malnutrition) and (starvation/starvashion).

Rose loves the color (fusha/fuchsia).

Please tell the (chauffeur/showffeur) to pick me up at nine o'clock.

38. Recognize all the possible spellings for the sound *th*

Th is another one of the English language's special compound consonants. The two letters *t* and *h* together almost always take on the specific pronunciation *th*.

There are two different sound variations of the compound consonant *th*. See if you can tell the difference between the long and the short pronunciations in the examples below.

EXAMPLES: **th**in, too**th**, wi**thh**old
then, smoo**th**, **th**ey

Practice saying both sets of words out loud a few times, so you can hear the difference. The first example set above is short *th* sounds; the second example set is long *th* sounds.

SPELLCHECK

Identify which th *sounds are long and which are short in the following sentence.*

This Thursday there will be thousands of stars worth watching.

39. Know that *gh* can sound like *f* or be silent

The double consonant configuration *gh* is often pronounced *ff* when found at the end of a word (see Rule 20). These words do not seem to make sense phonetically, meaning that they are not spelled as they sound, so it may be easiest to simply memorize the spellings of such *gh* words.

EXAMPLES: enou**gh**
tou**gh**
rou**gh**
cou**gh**

Gh can also be silent, as in *through*, *borough*, and *thought* (see Rule 21). In these words, the *gh* acts as an extension of the vowel sound preceding it and does not take on an *ff* pronunciation.

SPELLCHECK

Choose the correct spellings in the following sentences.

The child (caut/caught) a cold that resulted in a nasty (coff/cough).

Have you had (enough/enuff) to eat?

The gang members were treading on (tuff/tough) (turf/turgh).

40. Do not confuse *ph* with *f*

The double consonant configuration *ph* is almost always pronounced *ff* (see Rule 20). This is true for words that begin, end, and contain the letters *ph*. Being familiar with the pronunciations and spellings of the following examples will help you detect spelling errors and will also enable you to pronounce such words without difficulty.

EXAMPLES: gra**ph**
pharmacy
phosp**h**ate
phantom
philoso**ph**y
photogra**ph**y

SPELLCHECK

Locate the misspelled words and indicate whether a ph *or an* f *should be used.*

phonetic
feasant
physical
fenomenal
phantasy

41. Don't forget the silent *h* at the beginnings of some words

Some spellers forget that the silent *h*s can hide at the beginnings of words that sound as if they begin with vowels. There are several such words in the English language.

EXAMPLES: **heir**
honor
hour

Cockney English is one dialect that constantly leaves *h*s off the beginnings of words, even if they aren't silent. The sentence "How heavy is his head?" would be pronounced "Ow evvy is is ed?" While most American speakers don't have to worry about this, they do have to recognize when the *h* is present *and* silent. Without it, words such as *herbal* and *homage* would look very funny.

In addition, spellers should recognize that an *h* at the beginning of a word and in front of a *u*, as in *hubris*, is always pronounced. The *h* does not necessarily change the sound of the *u* pronunciation, however, as evident in the short *u* sound in *hum*.

SPELLCHECK

Choose the correct spelling in the following sentences.

Abraham Lincoln is still celebrated for his (honesty/onesty).

I detest hot and (umid/humid) weather.

He was one tough (hombre/ombre).

42. Know the adage *I* before *E* . . .

Words containing *ie* in the middle have plagued even the most proficient of spellers for what seems like an eternity. While the *I* before *E* rhyming has become the most clichéd spelling rule in the English language, it also continues to hold the most relevance. The reason for all of the difficulty may be explained by the fact that there are nearly as many exceptions to the rule as there are basic examples. Thus the only way to conquer the *I* before *E* syndrome is to first memorize the words that follow the standard logic:

EXAMPLES: ach**ie**ve
believe
f**ie**ld
fr**ie**nd
n**ie**ce
p**ie**ce

SPELLCHECK

Repeat these words to yourself five times and then spell them out loud five times. When you're done, note that in all six words above, the i *is preceded by a consonant other than* c.

43. Know the exceptions to *I* before *E* . . .

> " . . . Except after *C*
> Or when sounded like *ay*
> As in *neighbor* and *weigh*."

These are the two main exceptions to the basic *I* before *E* rule. The first, "Except after *C*," only means that if the *ie* combination follows the consonant *C*, the order becomes *ei*.

EXAMPLES: Memorize these common *ei* words and remember that in all of these cases, the *ei* follows the letter *c*.
ceiling
deceive
receipt
receive

Repeat the words to yourself and then spell them out loud five times.

The other exception to the rule is "Or when sounded like *ay*." There is a rule you can follow to find some of these words, since many of them include the silent *gh* combination. In other words, the *ei*, when formed with *gh*, is pronounced as an *ay* sound.

EXAMPLES: Memorize the common *eigh* words.
eight
freight
inveigh
neighbor

> **sleigh**
> **weigh**

Repeat the words to yourself and then spell them out loud five times.

There are also several words this rule applies to that do not involve an *eigh* pattern. These too should be memorized.

EXAMPLES: **deign**
              feign
              heinous
              inveigle
              reign
              rein
              skein
              vein

EXCEPTIONS: Of course, English wouldn't be English if it didn't have some words that are complete exceptions. Once again, memorization is the way to go.
              caffeine
              counterfeit
              forfeit
              surfeit
              either
              neither
              foreign
              sovereign
              heifer
              heir
              leisure
              protein
              seize
              sheikh (note that this can also be pronounced *ay*)

veil
weir
weird

SPELLCHECK

Identify the misspelled words (if any) in the following sentences.

When Joe bought the paper, he forgot to pick up the reciept.

Heidi also considers her neice her best friend.

Do you believe she could have decieved us?

Tina loves to ride on her sleigh with her nieghbor.

Emily ate a piece of pie yesterday.

Please return my call at your leasure.

James must forfeit the boxing tournament.

Her insomnia is directly related to her caffiene intake.

Do not use the fraight elevator.

The librarian enjoys peace and quiet only after the library closes.

44. Do not forget the silent *e*

One very important kind of letter pattern to be aware of is how words end. Remember that very few English words end in the letters *i, u,* or *v.* They are generally followed by a silent *e.* This applies to both root words and suffixes. So, when you are sounding a word out, and it seems to end in one of these sounds, don't forget the silent *e.*

EXAMPLES:	-**ie**s (suffix)	c**ue**	ha**ve**
	pie	d**ue**	sal**ve**
	vie	gl**ue**	-si**ve** (suffix)

Of course, there are some exceptions, but they represent other facts about English as a language. They tend to be of two types: They are either abbreviations that have come to be accepted as words, or words from other languages that have been adopted into English relatively recently.

EXCEPTIONS:
min**i** (from *miniskirt*)   em**u** (the Australian bird)
sk**i** (from Norwegian)   ecr**u** (from French)
tax**i** (from *taxicab*)   gur**u** (from Hindi)

SPELLCHECK

List all the words you can think of that end with -ie, -ue, *or* -ve. *If you really want a workout, try to come up with more exceptions (words ending in* -i,-u, *or* -v*).*

45. Remember that very few English words end in the letter *j*

Another ending you almost never see in English is the letter *j*. That sound is usually formed by a combination of letters, either -*ge* or -*dge* (see Rule 22). If you are sounding words out and you encounter this sound, again remember your silent final *e*.

EXAMPLES:
bu**dge**	a**ge**	colle**ge** .
ca**dge**	gor**ge**	gara**ge** .
he**dge**	hu**ge**	marria**ge**

The only exceptions to this rule come from India.

EXCEPTIONS: ra**j**   ta**j**

SPELLCHECK

List at least a dozen words that end with either -ge *or* -dge. *Award yourself extra credit if you can think of any other words that end in* -j.

46. Know that in American English, the æ and œ forms are almost never required

One of the holdovers from Latin that you still see every now and then in English is the connected pairing of the two vowels *a* and *e* as *æ*, as well as the connection of the vowels *o* and *e* as *œ*. The connection of two letters to form one is known as a ligature. When writing, know that in American English these forms are almost never required, and can be replaced simply by *e*. British English, however, still requires their use (see Rule 3), and many older books and publications using them are still around, so you should be able to recognize them when you see them.

EXAMPLES: encyclopædia—encyclopedia
hæmoglobin—hemoglobin
pædiatrics—pediatrics
œsophagus—esophagus

EXCEPTIONS: The main exception has to do with forms of the word *aesthetic*, which generally still use both the *a* and the *e*, although they are generally not linked as above. *Esthetic* is a variant spelling that is becoming more accepted, but it is not yet preferred. The other exceptions are words such as *Gaelic* (see Rule 11), but again these are not linked anymore either.

When joining prefixes to base words, keep in mind that prefixes do not affect the spelling of the root word. One of the most basic rules states that if the last letter of the prefix is the same as the first letter of the base word, there will be a double letter when the two are joined. The converse is also true: If the last letter of the prefix is not the same as the first letter of the base word, there will not be a double letter there. This sounds complicated, but it's actually quite simple, as the examples show.

EXAMPLES: dis + solve = dissolve
             inter + rupt = interrupt
             un + natural = unnatural

             dis + trust = distrust
             inter + national = international
             un + happy = unhappy

Notice that this rule only applies to double letters that appear where the prefix joins the base. It says nothing about double letters that might appear elsewhere in the base word, such as the double *p* in "happy" above.

SPELLCHECK

Think of at least half a dozen more examples of double letters created by the joining of prefixes, and half a dozen examples where no double letter is created.

48. When you add a prefix to a word, sometimes the prefix will change to match the first letter of the base word

The second basic rule for attaching prefixes to base words states that sometimes the prefix will change to match the first letter of the base word, so once again there will be a double letter when the two are joined. This sounds scarier than it really is, especially when you realize that the prefix *in-* (meaning "not something," or "in/into/on something") is the only one that does this. Occasionally the prefix will change, not to create a double letter, but to make the resulting word easier to pronounce (for example, "imbibe" rather than "inbibe").

In- can appear as *ig-*, *il-*, *im-*, *in-*, or *ir-*, depending on what letters it precedes. Unfortunately, there are exceptions in every case.

EXAMPLES: (1) *ig-* before a few words beginning with *n* (all are exceptions to words that would normally take *in-*)
ig + noble = ignoble
ig + nominy = ignominy
ig + norant = ignorant

(2) *il-* before words beginning with *l*
il + legal = illegal
il + legible = illegible

EXCEPTIONS: inland
inlay
inlet

83

(3) *im-* before words beginning with *b*, *m*, or *p*

im + balance = imbalance
im + becile = imbecile
im + mature = immature
im + mobile = immobile
im + perfect = imperfect
im + potent = impotent

EXCEPTIONS: inborn
inbred
inmate
inmost
inpatient
input

(4) *in-* before all other letters (including *n*)

in + ability = inability
in + finite = infinite
in + tangible = intangible

in + nate = innate
in + nocence = innocence
in + novation = innovation
in + nuendo = innuendo
in + numerable = innumerable

(5) *ir-* before words beginning with *r*

ir + rational = irrational
ir + regular = irregular

EXCEPTIONS: inroad
inrush

SPELLCHECK

Choose the correct spelling in the following sentences.

This is an (ilegitimate/illegitimate) excuse.

Many (immigrant/imigrant) workers join the Federation.

Being a brilliant musician is an (inate/innate) capability for Heather.

49. Know that when you add _all-_ to the beginning of a word as a prefix, you only use one _l_

Keep in mind that prefixes and suffixes can both change their spellings when they join up with words. This usually happens to make the resulting words easier to pronounce, or to avoid some sort of confusion that might otherwise result. One such change is that when you add _all-_ to the beginning of a word as a prefix, you only use one _l_.

EXAMPLES: all + mighty = almighty
all + most = almost
all + one = alone
all + ready = already
all + so = also
all + though = although
all + together = altogether
all + ways = always

You must also remember that two of the above combinations mean different things when they are left as two words.

Already is an adverb that has to do with time, referring to something that has happened. "I got to the vet as fast as I could, but Eliza had _already_ had her kittens." _All ready_ is a phrase that means completely prepared. "Is he _all ready_ to go?"

All together refers to a group of things, which are all in one place. Other words can appear between the _all_ and the _together_, and the meaning will not change. "Will the kittens _all_ stay _together_, or will the litter be split up?" *Altogether* means "completely" or "all things considered." It is one word, and cannot be split. "*Altogether* Eliza's speech went well, even though I wasn't able to be there." "The party afterward was *altogether* a success." (It also has a colloquial meaning of "naked," as in "I was in my *altogether* when the doorbell rang.")

There is another *all* + combination which deserves some mention here, and that is *all right*. Following the above rule, you would get "alright." Many people do indeed use this, but many others frown upon it as substandard. The safe course is to avoid it. If you are certain that your audience would approve, or if you are writing something very casual (such as a personal letter), go ahead, but otherwise stick with the accepted form.

SPELLCHECK

Make sure that all the words beginning with the prefix all- *are both spelled and used correctly in the following sentences. (Pay special attention to the words that mean different things when attached or not.)*

1. "I really think that NPR would have many more listeners if they'd named their program 'In the All Together' instead of 'All Things Considered.' "

2. Andrew allmost stayed home alone tonight, but then he went out to the gym.

3. All though she looked bad, she wasn't; Jessica was just drawn that way.

4. We like to play with cats, and we also like to tease the nasty little dog downstairs.

5. You're allways blinking your eyes.

50. Know the difference between the prefixes *ante-* and *anti-*

There is one pair of prefixes that causes endless trouble when people try to sound words out, and that is *ante-/anti-*. The problem is that they sound alike, but their meanings are quite different.

If you want to spell a word and you're not sure which prefix to use, stop and think about what you want to say. If you want to talk about something that is before something else, you want to use *ante-*. If you are discussing something that is against something, you need to use *anti-*. Unfortunately, the prefix *anti-* is so much more common than *ante-* that many people forget all about the possible alternative meaning.

One of the clearest examples of this confusion can be seen with the words *antebellum* and *antiwar*. They both sound as though they refer to feelings against war, but they don't. *Antiwar* does, but *antebellum* means before the war (specifically the Civil War, according to convention).

SPELLCHECK

Think of at least five more words that begin with the prefix ante-.

51. Know how to spell words beginning with *equi-*

Another prefix that causes spelling trouble is *equi-*. People tend to remember what it means (equality; see Rule 8), but they forget what vowel it takes in any given word. This can be tough because you often can't hear it when you try to sound it out.

A helpful hint is that when you are using the word *equal* with its precise original meaning—items that are the same in quantity, size, etc.—it is usually spelled with an *a* (as in *equality*, *equable*, or *equanimity*). If you are using the prefix to create a word that is further away from the original meaning, the vowel is more likely to be *i*. This is only a rule of thumb, but it can be of great assistance.

EXAMPLES: equidistant
               equilateral
               equivalent

SPELLCHECK

Choose the correct spelling in the following sentences.

There are (equally/equilly) as many men as women in the class.

He answered with (unequivocal/unequavocal) certainty and gusto.

The next vernal (equanox/equinox) will take place on March 23.

52. Remember that when you are using the prefix *ex-* to mean "former," it should always be hyphenated

The prefix *ex-* can mean "out of," but it can also mean "former." When it means "former," it should always be hyphenated when it is attached to its base word. This necessary separation is one reason it has taken on a life of its own as an abbreviation (someone talking about his or her "ex").

EXAMPLES: ex-baseball star
ex-husband
ex-wife

SPELLCHECK

Determine the proper spelling for the words in italics.

That is an *ex-cellent* comment.

My *x-girlfriend* still calls me twice a day.

Ted does not relish the thought of becoming Nicole's *exfiance.*

53. Know when to use the prefix *for-* and when to use the prefix *fore-*

Many people find themselves in a tangle when they try to spell a word beginning with *for-* or *fore-*, but they needn't. This is another case where meaning has a lot to do with spelling. *Fore-* means "before," "in front," or "beforehand"; *for-* means "not," "against," "away," or "utterly." Think carefully about the meaning of the word you are trying to spell, since it should tell you what prefix to use.

EXAMPLES: forehead
foresee
foreshadow
foretell

forbid
forlorn
forsake

EXCEPTION: foreclose

Of course, if you're not sure of the meaning involved, it doesn't hurt to know a couple of hints. First of all, the prefix *fore-* is much more common than *for-*. If you have to guess, go for *fore-*. Moreover, *for-* has become outdated and is no longer being used to create words, while *fore-* is.

SPELLCHECK

Choose the correct spelling in the following sentences.

Given a choice, Robert would never (forgo/forego) dessert.

She resolved to carry on with (forbearance/forebearance).

Her (forbears/forebears) arrived on the *Mayflower*.

If you wear that swimsuit, we will be forced to (forefeit/forfeit) the race.

I must have (foregotten/forgotten) to empty the trash before vacation.

54. To form the plurals of most nouns, just add -s

The formation of plurals may drive people crazy, but there is always one basic rule to fall back on to form the plurals of most nouns: Just add -s. (It helps to remember that a noun is a word representing a person, place, thing, or idea.)

EXAMPLES: teacher + s = teachers
hedgehog + s = hedgehogs
mountain + s = mountains
pencil + s = pencils
death + s = deaths

For compound nouns (nouns made up of two or more words), the last word is the one that takes the final -s when plural.

EXAMPLES: amusement park + s = amusement parks
hot-water bottle + s = hot-water bottles
swimming pool + s = swimming pools

This doesn't sound so complicated, but occasionally people do get mixed up, especially when adding the suffix -ful.

EXAMPLE: If the doctor gives you a spoonful of nasty cough medicine, and then a second one, you have two *spoonfuls* to face, not two "spoonsful."

Naturally, there are exceptions to this rule, which are frequent enough to earn their own rules (see Rules 55 through 60).

SPELLCHECK

Choose the correctly spelled plural nouns in the following sentences.

This class is a group of budding (anthropologistes/anthropologists).

Instead of just one handful of sugar, I fed the pony two big (handfuls/handsful).

(Runner's/Runners) must train for years to become Olympic-level athletes.

55. To form the plurals of nouns ending in a sibilant sound (*ch, sh, s, x, z*), add -*es*

There are times when sound can help your spelling, and this is one of them. When you need to form the plurals of nouns ending in a sibilant sound (*ch, sh, s, ss, x, z*), add -*es*.

EXAMPLES: beach + es = beaches
crash + es = crashes
bias + es = biases
gas + es = gases (*gasses* is also acceptable)
loss + es = losses
tax + es = taxes
whiz + es = whizzes

Note that when you add -*es* to a word ending in -*z* or -*s*, you usually double the final consonant.

For many of these words, the plural noun form is identical to the verb form, so to avoid trouble think carefully about how you want to use a word in a given sentence. Are you referring to a thing (noun), or to the performance of an action (verb)?

EXAMPLES: Don't you hate it when your computer *crashes*? (verb)
David was in three separate car *crashes* last year. (noun)

SPELLCHECK

Correct the misspelled words in italics.

Jenny is frightened of *witchs* and goblins, especially in late October.

The bee's *buzzs* started to annoy me as I tried to fall asleep.

The pile of *fax's* on his desk was growing larger and larger.

Neatly trimmed *bushs* lining the front walkway make that house look so inviting.

56. Know how to form the plurals of most nouns ending in -f, -ff, or -fe

There are a couple of things to keep in mind when you form the plurals of most nouns ending in -f or -ff. In most cases, you just add -s. For most nouns ending in -f or -fe, you change the final -fe to -ve, and then add -s.

EXAMPLES: roof + s = roofs
handkerchief + s = handkerchiefs
cliff + s = cliffs
cuff + s = cuffs
knife = knives
loaf = loaves
shelf = shelves

However, there are some common exceptions you need to watch out for. The good news here is that in several cases, both the regular form and the irregular are acceptable, so it's hard to go wrong.

EXCEPTIONS: safe—safes
hoof—hoofs or hooves
scarf—scarfs or scarves
wharf—wharfs or wharves

SPELLCHECK

Form the plural of the following nouns.

one calf: two_____

one wife: two_____

one dwarf: seven_____

57. Know how to form the plurals of nouns ending in -o

This is the rule that embarrassed former vice-president Dan Quayle, when he famously misspelled the word *potato*. Quayle's real tragedy was that he actually remembered part of the rule, but he applied it incorrectly! Here's how to avoid these errors.

To form the plural of most nouns ending in -o (or -oo) just add -s. For most nouns in which the -o is preceded by a consonant, add -es.

EXAMPLES: tattoo + s = tattoos
     radio + s = radios
     cameo + s = cameos

As it happens, there are relatively few -o words that take -es as a preferred spelling; the problem is that they are among the most common.

EXAMPLES:

buffalo — buffaloes	lingo — lingoes
cargo — cargoes	mango — mangoes
dingo — dingoes	Negro — Negroes
domino — dominoes	no — noes
echo — echoes	potato — potatoes
embargo — embargoes	tomato — tomatoes
go — goes	torpedo — torpedoes
hero — heroes	veto — vetoes
hobo — hoboes	volcano — volcanoes

Just to complicate matters further, there are some
-o words that can take either an -s or -es. Whether
-s or -es is used in these cases depends upon which
style your school or workplace prefers; the important
thing is to be consistent within each work.

EXAMPLES: archipelago(e)s   memento(e)s
           banjo(e)s   mosquito(e)s
           desperado(e)s   motto(e)s
           fiasco(e)s   peccadillo(e)s
           flamingo(e)s   portico(e)s
           grotto(e)s   salvo(e)s
           halo(e)s   tornado(e)s
           innuendo(e)s   virago(e)s
           lasso(e)s   zero(e)s
           manifesto(e)s

SPELLCHECK

Determine whether to use an e *for the italicized plurals in the following sentences.*

You like *potato(e)s*, I like *tomato(e)s*.

There were two yeses and three *no(e)s*.

Why does Miriam have two *cello(e)s*?

58. Know how to form the plurals of nouns ending in -y

The last group of nouns that tend to be troublemakers in spelling are those that end in -y. Fortunately, the rules for dealing with them are fairly simple. To form the plurals of most nouns ending in -y, change the y to an i and add -es. For most nouns in which the y is preceded by a vowel, keep the y and add -s.

EXAMPLES: berry—berries
fancy—fancies
lady—ladies
oddity—oddities

convoy—convoys
donkey—donkeys

SPELLCHECK

Choose the correct spelling in the following sentences.

The team holds at least two pep (rallies/rally's) per season.

Ms. Hudson generates so much paperwork that she employs two (secretarys/secretaries).

Children with so many (toys/toies) should be very thankful.

59. Know that some words form their plurals according to their original language

Many of the irregularities in English arise from our freewheeling approach to taking words from other languages. These words often then follow the rules of the original language when forming plurals rather than the rules of English. Fortunately, you can often tell which words are going to cause such problems, since they contain letter patterns that are not normally part of English.

EXAMPLES: beau—beaux (from the French)
criterion—criteria (from the Latin)
datum—data (also from the Latin)

The word *data* reveals another common problem caused by our linguistic theft, and that is the use of plural forms as singular. This is particularly common in the case of the words *criteria* and *data*, but it happens to other words as well.

SPELLCHECK

Now that you've read all the rules for making nouns plural, look around the room. For the next five minutes, write down the plural of everything that you see.

60. Beware of irregular plural forms

Some of the most well-known pitfalls in the English language occur in the area of irregular plural forms. People learning English as a second or third language marvel at the seeming arbitrariness of it all: "How do you remember all this?" is a frequent question, generally asked in a tone of complete exasperation.

The preceding rules have given you a rational way to approach many irregularities. The problem is that many words are so irregular that there are no rules; there's nothing left but case-by-case memorization.

EXAMPLES: ox—oxen
goose—geese
moose—moose
tooth—teeth
foot—feet
mouse—mice
louse—lice
house—houses

As you can tell from the above list of examples, among the worst trouble areas are animal names. (The collective nouns used to refer to animals are just as bad, from a vocabulary point of view: a gaggle of geese, a school of fish, and so on.)

If it's any comfort, linguists argue that when children acquire language, they tend to learn the rules first, and their mistakes involve over-applying them. Students should not change this approach, but simply be aware early on of the existence of irregular

plural forms, to know how to deal with them before
they become a problem.

SPELLCHECK

*Since irregular plurals are difficult to memorize, take
a few minutes to come up with ways to remember
these plurals. See Rule 100 for more information on
memory devices.*

Singular	Plural
alumna	alumnae
alumnus	alumni
appendix	appendixes, appendices
basis	bases
brother	brothers, brethren
oasis	oases
opus	opera, opuses
ox	oxen
radius	radii

61. Know how to form the comparative and superlative forms of adjectives

Unlike nouns, which are words that represent things, adjectives modify, or describe words. Many adjectives change their spelling to allow different levels of description. When you compare two things, you use the comparative form of an adjective. You are saying that while something has a certain quality to it, a second something has more of that quality. For adjectives of one syllable, add *-er* to form the comparative. If the word already ends in *-e*, you just add *-r*.

EXAMPLES: rich + er = richer
           dumb + er = dumber
           blue + r = bluer

Of course, a quality could refer to a lack of something, so in such cases the comparative means the second has even less. For example, if I didn't have very much money, but you had even less, I would be *poor*, but you would be *poorer*.

If you are comparing three or more things, you use the superlative form, which shows the end of the comparison, by describing the thing that has the most of whatever is being discussed.

For adjectives of one syllable, the superlative is usually formed by adding *-est* to the end of an adjective. As with the comparative form, if the word already ends with *-e*, you just add *-st*.

EXAMPLES: tall + est = tallest
           clever + est = cleverest
           white + st = whitest

For adjectives of two or more syllables—other than
those ending in *-y* (see Rule 62)—the spelling doesn't
usually change. Instead, you use the words *more*
(comparative) or *most* (superlative) before the adjective. *Clever* is one of the few exceptions to the rule.

SPELLCHECK

*In the following sentences, fill in the comparative and
superlative forms of the word in italics.*

Professor East is *intellectual*; his wife is even
_____. Theirs is the_____lifestyle I know.

The first song was *loud*, but the second song was
_____. The_____by far was the fifth song.

Linda's hair is *short*. Mine is_____, but Joe has
the_____hair of us all.

62. Know how to form the comparative and superlative forms of adjectives that end in -y

Adjectives that end in -y have to be treated a little differently from other adjectives. In English, the letter y, when acting as a vowel, cannot be followed by another vowel, so you have to follow a slightly different rule when forming your comparatives and superlatives. Fortunately, it's quite simple: For adjectives ending in -y, change the y to an i, then add -er to form the comparative and -est for the superlative. However, if the adjective has a vowel before the -y, the -y remains.

EXAMPLES: gray—grayer—grayest
             happy—happier—happiest
             sunny—sunnier—sunniest

*EXCEPTIONS: shy—shyer—shyest
              sly—slyer—slyest
              spry—spryer—spryest
              wry—wryer—wryest

*Note that these are the preferred spellings. Using the letter i (i.e., shier, shiest) is also acceptable.

SPELLCHECK

Think of your three favorite movie stars (or musicians, or writers, or some such grouping). Think of five adjectives to describe your favorite. Then, compare the three, changing the adjectives accordingly.

EXAMPLE: Cary Grant was the perfect movie star. He
was *handsome, intelligent, suave, articulate,* and *sexy.* I like him better than more
modern stars such as Marlon Brando or
John Travolta, because . . .

63. Know how to form regular adverbs and recognize irregular ones

Adverbs are words that modify, or describe, verbs, adjectives, and other adverbs. The good thing about adverbs is that it's quite simple to spell the regular ones. The bad thing is that there are quite a few irregular ones, which have to be memorized.

The basic rule for forming adverbs is this: Add -*ly* to the base word. If the base word already ends in -*y*, you change the *y* to an *i* and then add the -*ly*.

EXAMPLES: quick + ly = quickly
sad + ly = sadly
busy = busily

In spoken usage, people often forget to add the -*ly*. However, when writing, it doesn't make your work look colloquial or casual to omit it; it merely makes it look sloppy.

INCORRECT: Jane was *real* tired after her first day of work as a proofreader.
CORRECT: Jane was *really* tired after her first day of work as a proofreader.

Some of the most common adverbs are the irregular ones. Memorizing them sounds scary, until you realize you already know most (if not all) of them.

EXAMPLES: almost   not
already   nowhere

always	only
before	quite
how	so
just	too
less	very
little	well
more	when
much	where
never	why
no	yes

SPELLCHECK

Find all the adverbs in the following sentences, and fix the spelling wherever necessary.

I saw a bicycle accident today that almost ended very *bad*.

If we run *quick* to the store and buy a new one, Dad will never know that we blew up a box of eggs in the microwave.

It's difficult to knit *gracefully* while wearing mittens.

The pitcher threw his slow curve too *slow*, and the batter hit it out of the park.

Phil ran out the door *hurriely*.

64. Adjectives ending in -*le* don't add -*ly* to form adverbs; they just change the final -*e* to -*y*

One of the basic ideas in language is that of economy; you only make changes if you really have to. As you know, most adverbs are formed by adding -*ly* to an adjective. However, adjectives that end in -*le* save themselves the trouble of adding -*ly* to form adverbs; they just change the final -*e* to -*y*.

EXAMPLES: double—doubly
simple—simply
subtle—subtly

SPELLCHECK

See how many more words you can find that follow this rule.

65. Know how to form comparative and superlative forms of adverbs.

Like adjectives, adverbs can be used to compare things. There are three degrees of comparison with adverbs: the positive, the comparative, and the superlative. There are two basic ways to form comparison adverb forms. First, if the adverb doesn't end in -*ly*, just add -*er* to form the comparative; add -*est* to form the superlative.

EXAMPLES: soon   sooner   soonest
            fast   faster   fastest

    Secondly, if the adverb does end in -*ly*, you need to use the modifiers *more* or *less* to form the comparative, and the modifiers *most* and *least* to form the superlative. Luckily, the spelling of the root word (also known as the positive form of the adverb) does not change at all for either the comparative or the superlative.

EXAMPLES:

simply	more simply	most simply
nicely	more nicely	most nicely
abruptly	less abruptly	least abruptly

SPELLCHECK

Choose the correct spelling in the following sentences.

Andy edited his work the (most carefulliest/most carefully).

The youngest ballerina plodded on to the stage most (gracelessly/gracelessley).

We are (nearier/nearer) to our destination than we were this morning.

66. Beware of double consonants

Double consonants have caused more than their share of trouble for spellers. Sometimes they are created at the beginning of words (see Rules 47, 48, and 49); sometimes they appear at the end of words (see Rules 67 and 68); and sometimes they appear in the middle. The letter *l* causes different problems entirely (see Rule 93).

In general, double consonants appear in the middle of words to control the sounds of vowels. Take the word *middle* from the previous sentence. If it only had one *d*, the short *i* sound would be lengthened (it would be pronouncd my'dle instead of mid'dle). Sounding words out is the best way to think about double consonants that are part of root words.

As with many other things in life, once you know what problems to look out for, half the battle is won. Studying the rules regarding double consonants will at least help you look out for the problem. See Rule 89 for the most commonly misspelled double consonants.

SPELLCHECK

Check the spelling of all words in the following sentences, paying special attention to words with double consonants.

I'm looking forward to rereading *Stuart Little* tommorow.

Skinhound was delighted to be named a Felow of his college.

Mery New Year and Happy Christmas, everyone!

Did you setle your quarel with your ex?

67. Know when to double the final consonant when you add suffixes

The first thing to realize when adding a suffix is that when the suffix begins with a consonant, the final consonant of the root word remains single.

EXAMPLES: wish + ful = wishful
doubt + less = doubtless
quick + ly = quickly
ship + ment = shipment
slow + ness = slowness

For suffixes that begin with vowels, there is a rule. It sounds a bit complicated, but it's harder to state than to follow:

If the root word ends in a single consonant,
if the consonant is preceded by a single vowel sound written with a single letter, and
if the vowel is stressed,
then the final consonant is doubled.
If any one of these conditions is not met, then the consonant is not doubled.

"Huh?" you say. Some examples should make this a bit clearer.

Take the word *control*. Let's say you want to add the suffix *-ing*. The question is, Do you double the final consonant, or not? Test *control* against the rule given above. First of all, it does end in a single consonant. Next, the last syllable does have a single vowel sound, and it is spelled with only one letter (the second *o*). Finally, that vowel is stressed, meaning that it is the sound you emphasize when you say the word. Since all the "if" conditions are met, the rule says that yes, you should double the final *l*, and that is correct. The word you want to spell is *controlling*.

Let's do another. Try the word *gleam*, this time, and add the suffix *-ed*. It does end in a single consonant, so it meets the first condition. It only has one vowel sound, so that must be the one being stressed. But, that vowel sound is spelled with two letters, *ea*, and the rule says that if you are to double the consonant, the vowel sound has to be spelled with only one letter. So, you don't double the consonant: *gleamed*.

There are two points that you have to keep in mind with this rule. The first has to do with the letter *q*. In English, *q* is always followed by *u*; this rule is so strong that the *u* counts as a consonant for the purposes of the consonant doubling rules. Therefore, in the word *quit*, even though it looks as though there are two vowels, only one counts. Since *quit* meets all the other conditions listed above, the final *t* is doubled in words like *quitter* or *quitting*.

Second, you should remember that even if a consonant is silent in a word, it still counts for this rule. Since *delight* ends in three consonants (even though it only sounds as though it ends in one), it fails the first condition of the doubling rule. So, you don't double the final consonant in *delighted*.

Either a single *h* or a single *w* at the end of a word is an exception to this; neither counts as a consonant, so neither is doubled.

EXCEPTIONS: hoorah + ing = hoorahing
follow + ing = following

Unfortunately, there are several other notable exceptions, which are numerous enough to require their own rule (see Rule 68). For more on double *t*, see Rule 29.

SPELLCHECK

Using the above rule, test the words below and make sure the consonants are doubled when (and only when) they should be.

Stephen was tirred of writting all night long.

I can't wait to see the next issue of *Vogue Knitting*.

You're not only unforgettable, you're unavoiddable.

Chris loved droping water balloons onto the crowded street.

I didn't think people were allowwed to smoke in phone booths.

68. Know when not to double the final consonant when you add suffixes

Naturally, there are many exceptions to the basic rule about doubling consonants when adding suffixes. They can be grouped by the letters or syllables they affect.

The final consonant of a compound word—(a word made by combining two or more shorter words)—is always doubled, regardless of the stress pattern the compound has created, if it would be doubled when not in a compound.

EXAMPLE: brim—brimmed, brimming
         broad + brim + ed = broadbrimmed

There are also a few words that pretend they are compounds, and follow this rule.

EXAMPLES: hobnob—hobnobbed, hobnobbing
          humbug—humbuggery, humbugged
          zigzag—zigzagged, zigzagging

Most of the words that end in the syllable -*fer* follow the rules. However, when they are followed by the suffixes -*able* or -*ence*, the emphasis shifts from the -*fer* syllable to the first one, and so the final *r* is not doubled. In the word *transfer*, the emphasis does not shift, but the final *r* still isn't doubled.

EXAMPLES: confer—conferred, conferring, *but* conference

prefer—preferred, preferring, *but* preferable

transfer—transferred, transferring, *but* transference

Words that end in the syllable *-gram* always double the final *m* before a vowel, no matter where the emphasis goes.

EXAMPLES: program—programmed, programmer

In American English, most words ending in *-l* follow the basic rule given above, while in British English there are a great many exceptions, and the *-l* is usually doubled. However, there are some exceptions, even in American English. To begin with, the final *-l* in *parallel* is never doubled (as you can see in *unparalleled*).

Certain adjectives that end in *-ous* do not double their final *-l*.

EXAMPLES: miraculous
           perilous
           populous
           querulous
           ridiculous
           scandalous
           scurrilous

The final *-l* is not doubled before the following suffixes: *-ize*, *-ism*, *-ist*, and *-ity*.

EXAMPLES: civil—civility, civilize
           equal—equality, equalize
           final—finalist, finality, finalize
           normal—normality, normalize

There are a few verbs that end in *-p* for which the preferred spelling does not follow the main rule regarding doubling of final consonants.

EXAMPLES: handicap—handicapped, handicapping
kidnap—kidnapped, kidnapper, kidnap-
ping
worship—worshipped, worshipper, wor-
shipping

Since the letter *x* is pronounced *ks* in English when it falls at the end of a word, it counts as two consonants, not one. Thus, words that end in *-x* fail to meet the first condition of the rule for doubling consonants, and do not double the final *-x*.

EXAMPLES: box—boxed, boxer, boxing
mix—mixed, mixer, mixes, mixing
sex—sexes, sexy

Finally, there are a few words where you can use either a single or a double final consonant, and both are acceptable.

EXAMPLES: focus—focused or focussed
gas—gases or gasses
plus—pluses or plusses

SPELLCHECK

Test the words below against your knowledge of the rules and exceptions. Make sure the consonants are doubled when (and only when) they should be.

That rat of a dog maulled my husband's leg.

You don't look relaxed siting on those boxes of dynamite.

It's a shame so few people use personal caling cards anymore when visitting.

The tranquillity of the lake was disturbed only by that dreadful developper; he should be buggywhipped out of town.

Heather was so spoilled she only went swiming when she had the pool to herself.

69. Know when to end words with -*able*

Although sounding words out is generally a good idea, it can also lead to problems, especially when things sound alike. Many people get confused about whether a word should end with -*able* or -*ible*, for instance. There are a couple of rules that can help you know when to end words with -*able* (see Rule 70 for ending words with -*ible*).

If the word in question ends with either a hard *c* (pronounced as a *k*) or a hard *g* (pronounced as a *g*), it must end in -*able*. If it were to end with -*ible*, the *i* would soften the *c* and the *g* and change the pronunciation (to *s* and *j*, respectively).

EXAMPLES: amicable
despicable
implacable
navigable

· If the stem of the word makes up a complete English word in and of itself, the suffix is usually -*able*.

EXAMPLES: adapt + able = adaptable
break + able = breakable
fashion + able = fashionable
laugh + able = laughable
pay + able = payable

Unfortunately, keep in mind the fact that there are quite a few exceptions to these rules (see Rules 67, 68, 71, and 81–87).

SPELLCHECK ·

Think of ten more words that follow either of the rules given above.

70. Know when to end words with *-ible*

Both the *-able* and the *-ible* suffixes come from Latin. That language had its own rules about when the different forms should be used, but unfortunately those rules have not translated well into English, leaving us with a muddle. Here are a couple of rules that can help you identify words that end in *-ible* (see Rule 69 for words ending in *-able*).

If the stem of the word is not a complete English word, the suffix is usually *-ible*. Roots such as "aud," "cred," "elig," and "vis" are not words unto themselves, and therefore *-ible* is the appropriate suffix for them. This would produce the words *audible, credible, eligible,* and *visible*. Note how funny (and incorrect) *-able* would be at the end of these words (*audable, credable, eligable,* and *visable*).

If you can add *-ion* to the root word (not *-ation* or *-ition*, just *-ion*) and create a related word, then the correct suffix will most likely be *-ible*.

EXAMPLES: corrupt + ion = corruption : corrupt + ible = corruptible

interrupt + ion = interruption : interrupt + ible = interruptible

perfect + ion = perfection : perfect + ible = perfectible

Once again, there are unfortunately many exceptions to the above rules (see Rules 67, 68, 71, and 81–87).

SPELLCHECK

List half a dozen words that do follow the above rules.

71. Watch out for exceptions in words ending with *-able* or *-ible*

English being the language of exceptions, there are quite a few exceptions to the rules governing whether a word ends in *-able* or *-ible*. Perhaps the most helpful rule is this: Know that many more words end in *-able* than in *-ible*. If you must guess, odds are in *-able*'s favor.

Then again, remember that there a few words which waffle, and take either *-able* or *-ible*. These are annoying if you are the type of speller who goes by the look of a word, but they are marvelous if you are the type who cannot remember which ending to use.

EXAMPLES: collectable, or collectible
correctable, or correctible
detectable, or detectible

Here is a list of fifteen words that take *-ible* even though the rules say they should take *-able*.

EXCEPTIONS: collapsible forcible
contemptible gullible
convertible indestructible
convincible inflexible
deducible irresistible
discernible reducible
flexible responsible
sensible

Now, to be fair, here is a list of seventeen words that, according to the rules, end in *-ible* but actually end in *-able*.

EXCEPTIONS:

affable	inexorable
amenable	inscrutable
arable	malleable
culpable	memorable
equitable	palpable
formidable	predictable
indomitable	probable
ineffable	unconscionable
inevitable	vulnerable

SPELLCHECK

Figure out which rules the above exceptions are breaking.

72. Know when to end words with -*acy* or -*asy*

Another pair of endings that often causes trouble is -*acy* and -*asy*. Fortunately, keeping these straight is not terribly difficult. To begin with, there are very few words that end in -*asy*.

EXAMPLES: apost**asy**
ecst**asy**
fant**asy**
idiosyncr**asy**

Words ending in -*acy* are generally related to words ending in -*crat* or -*ate*.

EXAMPLES: aristocrat—aristocracy
bureaucrat—bureaucracy
democrat—democracy
delicate—delicacy
intimate—intimacy
private—privacy

Actually, the word people most often get confused about doesn't end with either -*acy* or -*asy*, although those are the common choices. The word most people mess up is hypoc**risy**. In that case, remembering the related forms of the word (see Rule 9) can help: They are *hypocritical* and *hypocrite*.

SPELLCHECK

See if you can list at least another ten words that end in -*acy*.

73. Know when to end words with -*ance*

Also problematic are the endings -*ance* and -*ence*. Two rules are included here that can help you know when to end words with -*ance* (see Rule 74 for words ending in -*ence*). The good news is that these rules also apply to words ending in -*ant* or -*ancy* (most of the time).

For starters, if the letter before the ending is a hard *c* or a hard *g* (pronounced *k* or *g*), then the word will end with -*ance*.

EXAMPLES: arrogance
elegance
significance

Exceptions occur when the *g* is a soft *j* sound. In those cases, an *i* or an *e* precedes the -*ance*, as in the two examples below.

EXAMPLES: allegiance
vengeance

Words that are related to verbs ending in -*ate* or nouns ending in -*ation* generally end in -*ance*.

EXAMPLES: domination—dominance
resonate—resonance
substantiate—substance
tolerate—tolerance

EXCEPTION: violate—violence

Nouns formed from verbs ending in *-ear, -ure,* or *-y* end in *-ance.* (see Rules 58 and 62 on spelling of words ending in *-y*).

EXAMPLES: appear — appearance
           forbear — forbearance
           assure — assurance

SPELLCHECK

Think of at least ten words that follow the above rules.

74. Know when to end words with -ence

Now you need to know when to end words with -ence.
Once again, there are some useful rules, and some
annoying exceptions. As with words ending in -ance,
-ant, and -ancy, these rules also apply (in most cases)
to words ending in -ent or -ency.

One good basic rule states that nouns formed from
verbs ending in -ere will end in -ence.

EXAMPLES: adhere—adherence
                cohere—coherence
                inhere—inherence
                interfere—interference

EXCEPTION: persevere—perseverance

Sound can give you some clues. If the letter before
the ending is a soft c or g (pronounced s or j), then
the word will end with -ence. Many of these words
have -isc- or -esc- in the second-to-last syllable.

EXAMPLES: adolescence
                effervescence
                intelligence
                negligence
                reminiscence
                reticence

There are also several syllables that are usually followed by -ence; these include -cid-, -fid-, -sid-,
-vid-, -flu-, -qu-, and -sist-.

EXAMPLES: incidence
                 confidence
                 subsidence
                 providence
                 influence
                 sequence
                 insistence

EXCEPTIONS: assistance
                   resistance

SPELLCHECK

Find as many more words as you can to fit the above patterns.

75. Know that there are eight words that end in either *-ant* or *-ent*, depending on whether they are being used as nouns or adjectives

There is a set of exceptions to all of the previous rules, and they refer to eight lucky words that can end in either *-ant* or *-ent*, depending on whether they are being used as nouns or adjectives. This distinction is blurring as time goes by, and dictionaries have begun to accept both forms, but for the sake of clarity you should know the rule (and the eight words involved).

NOUNS: dependant, descendant, pendant, and propellant

ADJECTIVES: dependent, descendent, pendent, and propellent

In other words, if a child depends on you, he or she is *dependent* on you (adjective), so you can claim him or her as a *dependant* on your tax forms (noun).

Of course, English being English, there is one word which is an exception to this exception: There is only one correct spelling for *independent*, no matter how it is used. If you do not belong to any political party, you are not only politically *independent*, (adjective), you are an *independent* (noun).

SPELLCHECK

Use each of the six remaining words in a sentence, and make sure you spell the word correctly for its use in that sentence.

76. Know when to end words with -ary, -ery, or -ory

Once again, thinking about the meaning of the word you want can help your spelling. For example, there are several ways you can tell when to end words with -ary, -ery, or -ory.

Verbs or "doer" nouns ending in -er are often related to words ending in -ery, while similar words ending in -ar or -or often end in -ary or -ory.

EXAMPLES: baker—bakery
          deliver—delivery
          director—directory
          burglar—burglary

Almost all of the words that end in -ery are nouns. Think about the word you want to spell: Is it a noun? If not, it probably won't end in -ery.

EXAMPLES: stationery: noun, a kind of writing paper
          stationary: adjective, meaning immobile

EXCEPTIONS: blistery
            blustery
            plastery
            splintery
            slippery

If you can replace the -ry ending with -ion and create another English word, then the correct ending is most likely -ory.

EXAMPLES: access + ion—accession; + ory—acces-
           sory
           direct + ion—direction; + ory—direc-
           tory

If the stem of a noun ending in *-ry* is a recognizable
English word, then the ending is most likely going
to be *-ery*. If not, it will probably be *-ory* or *-ary*.

EXAMPLES: cream—creamery
           debauch—debauchery

Notice that "vocabul" is not a word in English, nor
is "laborat" (vocabulary or laboratory).

EXCEPTIONS: dictionary
             honorary
             infirmary
             legionary
             missionary
             secretary
             tributary
             visionary
             artillery
             cemetery
             dysentery
             effrontery
             gallery

SPELLCHECK

*Check the endings of the words in the following sen-
tences.*

I want to be an acter when I grow up—or maybe a
singer.

Bonnie Prince Charlie was a Pretendar to the English throne.

Lindbergh was a great aviator.

DeLorenzo's Shoe Repair is the best bootery in my town.

That word is not in the dictionery.

Have you ever tried a sensary deprivation chamber?

Sometimes spelling changes occur for logical phonetic reasons, such as preserving particular sounds. One such change is that words ending in -*c* often add a *k* before suffixes beginning with *e, i,* or *y*, to protect the hard *c* (*k*) sound.

EXAMPLES: panic: panicking, panicked, panicky
picnic: picnicking, picnicked

EXCEPTIONS: arc
talc
zinc

Of course, if the word in question doesn't keep the hard *c* sound, no *k* is added.

EXAMPLES: critic + ize = criticize
italic + ize = italicize
domestic + ity = domesticity
electric + ity = electricity

SPELLCHECK

Choose the correctly spelled word in the following sentences.

The sight of puppies (frolicing/frolicking) makes me want to get a dog.

The couple was (picniccing/picnicking) at the river bend.

He may be arrested for (trafficing/trafficking) materials out of the country.

78. Know when words should end in -*ce* or -*se*

Another popular pitfall for spellers is recognizing when words should end in -*ce* or -*se*. Fortunately, there are several helpful rules to keep in mind.

Words that are pronounced with a *z* sound are spelled -*se* (see also Rule 91, on -*ise* vs. -*ize*).

EXAMPLES: advise
             devise
             exercise
             refuse (the verb)
             revise

Words that are pronounced with an *s* sound immediately following a vowel are spelled -*ce*.

EXAMPLES: advice
             device
             justice
             lice
             office
             voice

EXCEPTIONS: house
               louse
               mouse
               obtuse
               profuse
               refuse (the noun)

Words that are pronounced with an *s* sound following a consonant can be spelled with either an -*se* or a -*ce*. When in doubt, be aware that the -*ce* ending is far more common.

EXAMPLES: -*ce*   -*se*
           advance   endorse
           commence   recompense
           commerce   response
           dance   sense
           fence
           finance
           hence
           pence
           pronounce
           romance
           since

Adjectives ending in an *ens* sound are spelled -*se*.

EXAMPLES: dense
           immense
           tense

Nouns that are related to adjectives ending in either -*ant* or -*ent* are spelled with -*ce*.

EXAMPLES: absorbent — absorbence
           different — difference
           tolerant — tolerance

SPELLCHECK

Using the above rules, come up with ten more words that end in either -ce or -se.

79. Know which words end in -cede, -ceed, and -sede

People often get tangled trying to remember whether a given word ends in *-cede, -ceed*, or *-sede*. Fortunately, the rule here is actually quite clear: Most end in *-cede*.

EXAMPLES: accede
            precede
            recede

The good news is that there are only three words in English that end in *-ceed*.

EXAMPLES: exceed
            proceed
          , succeed

And the best news is that there is only one word in the English language that ends in *-sede*: supersede.

SPELLCHECK

Without looking at what you just read, list the only three -ceed *words in the English language. Next, see if you know the one word ending in* -sede.

80. Know when to spell words with *-ch* and when to spell them with *-tch*

As is often the case, people get confused when there is more than one way to represent a given sound. This often happens with *-ch* and *-tch*, since both of these spellings give a *ch* sound (see Rule 35). Luckily, there is a three-part rule that covers almost every instance where this choice arises.

(1) If the letter that precedes the *ch* sound is a consonant, use *-ch*.

EXAMPLES: arch
             branch
             torch

(2) If the letter that precedes the *ch* sound is a vowel sound written with a single letter, use *-tch*.

EXAMPLES: catch
             fetch
             watch

(3) If what precedes the *ch* sound is a vowel sound written with more than one letter, use *-ch*.

EXAMPLES: approach
             brooch
             mooch
             leech
             touch

EXCEPTIONS: There are only eleven English words
that do not fit this overall pattern. One,
the spelled-out name of the letter *h*,
adds a *t* after a double vowel, where it
doesn't belong (*aitch*), but all the others have *-ch* where a *-tch* would be ex-
pected.

attach
detach
enrich
much
ostrich
rich
sandwich
spinach
such
which

SPELLCHECK

*Following the above rule, come up with a list of at
least a dozen words ending with either -ch or -tch,
and spell them correctly.*

81. Know that when words end in -*e*, they generally drop the final -*e* before suffixes that begin with vowels and keep the final -*e* before suffixes that begin with consonants

How many spelling champions has the pesky final -*e* dethroned over the years? One shudders to think. The final -*e* plays an important part in the spelling of many words, since it often governs an earlier vowel, but the real trouble arises when words that end in -*e* have to be combined with suffixes. Sometimes it's easy, but all too often it's not.

There is one basic, fundamental rule: When words end in -*e*, they generally drop the final -*e* before suffixes that begin with vowels and keep the final -*e* before suffixes that begin with consonants.

EXAMPLES: note + able = notable
culture + al = cultural
guide + ance = guidance
adore + ation = adoration
admire + er = admirer
use + ful = useful
bubble + ing = bubbling
time + less = timeless
desire + ous = desirous
awe + some = awesome
safe + ty = safety
game + y = gamy

Sadly, there are a great many exceptions to this, so many that they have their own rules (which will be discussed in Rules 82 through 87).

SPELLCHECK

Look at the root word on the left, then choose the correctly spelled form of the word on the right.

Root Word	With Suffix
admire	(admireation/admiration)
love	(loving/loveing)
volume	(voluminous/volumeinous)

82. Do not drop the final -e before suffixes beginning with *a* or *o*

Among the many exceptions to the basic rule of when to keep or drop a final -e (see Rule 81), one says that in order to preserve soft *c* and *g* sounds (*s* and *j* sounds), the final -e should not be dropped before suffixes beginning with *a* or *o*.

·EXAMPLES: change—changeable
            courage—courageous
            peace—peaceable
            knowledge—knowledgeable

SPELLCHECK

Identify which of the words are misspelled in the following sentences (if any).

There was a noticeable change in water pressure when the plumber was changeing the pipes.

We didn't believe that the new law was enforcable in that neighborhood.

I questioned the interchangability of foreign and domestic parts.

Law enforcment is a crucial part of civil obedience.

83. Verbs ending in *-e* keep it, even before *-ing*, if necessary to distinguish between words that would otherwise look the same

There are times when spelling rules must bend for the sake of coherence and sanity, and this is one of those times. Verbs that end in *-e* keep their ending, even before an *-ing* suffix, if necessary to distinguish between words that would otherwise look the same. In other words, there are a few cases where dropping the final *-e* would create two identical words with different meanings. To avoid mass confusion, a little spelling confusion is preferable.

EXAMPLES: singe—singeing (as distinct from sing—singing)
tinge—tingeing (ting—tinging)

Fortunately, these are the only examples of this rule left in modern English (the other words it applied to have fallen into disuse).

84. Verbs which end in -ie change to a y before an -ing suffix

There are some spelling rules that do make sense, given certain fundamental rules of the language as a whole. For example, English does not generally recognize a double *i* as an acceptable letter pattern. (The few exceptions are always connected to recently imported words, such as the Norwegian *skiing*.) Thus, if verbs which end in *-ie* followed the basic rule of dropping the final *-e* before suffixes beginning with vowels, these verbs would have a double *i* whenever *-ing* was added. This is unacceptable, so we have this exception rule: Verbs that end in *-ie* change to a *y* before an *-ing* suffix.

EXAMPLES: die—dying
           lie—lying
           tie—tying

SPELLCHECK

For the following verbs, choose the correct spelling when the suffix -ing is added.

Root Word	With Suffix
lie	lying/lieing
vie	viing/vying
belie	belying/belieng

85. Verbs ending in *-oe*, *-ee*, and *-ye* keep the final *-e* before all suffixes except those beginning with *e*

The above rule holds true for the simple reason that the words would be almost impossible to say if you didn't follow this rule. You'd wind up with something unpronounceable, or simply non-English (such as a triple *e* combination).

EXAMPLES: agree—agreeing—agreeable, but agreed
dye—dyeing, but dyed
hoe—hoeing, but hoed

Imagine if there were no *e* exception to this rule. We would see words such as *she fleed* or *he examineed*. In the interest of avoiding verbal chaos, it has become necessary to modify such verbs when adding suffixes.

SPELLCHECK

Choose the correct spelling in the following sentences.

Our company (acceded/accedeed) to the merger with the large corporation.

The fire is slowly (dying/dieing).

Frank only (sees/seys) what he wants to believe.

86. Keep the final -e before the suffix -y in words that end in -ue, and a few other words

There is another time that you keep the final -e when you would not otherwise expect to, and that is before the suffix -y in words that end in -ue.

EXAMPLE: glue—gluey

You also hold onto the final -e with the following, random-seeming list of words (although alternate spellings that drop the -e have become acceptable in a few cases).

EXAMPLES: cage—cagey [alternate spelling *cagy* is acceptable]
dice—dicey
mate—matey
price—pricey [alternate spelling *pricy* is also acceptable]
nose—nosey [alternate spelling *nosy* is also acceptable]

Keep in mind that different spellings can change meanings: *Holy* means sacred, while *holey* means full of holes.

87. Exceptions regarding final -*e* that don't follow any of the earlier rules

Finally, there are a bunch of exceptions to all the rules regarding what to do with words ending in -*e*. These are grouped as follows.

(1) There are four adjectives that end in -*e* which have odd adverbial forms.

> due — duly
> true — truly
> eerie — eerily
> whole — wholly

(2) Some words have alternate spellings that are acceptable; the first is regular, the other irregular.

> cuing or cueing
> likable or likeable
> milage or mileage
> movable or moveable
> sizable or sizeable

(3) Some words are just exceptional.

> acreage, not acrage
> ageism, not agism
> awful, not aweful
> fledgling, not fledgeling
> ninth, not nineth

SPELLCHECK

You now know all the rules for dealing with words that end in -e. Go back through the rules, and find at least one more example for each case (except Rule 83).

88. Know which words end in -*ify* and which end in -*efy*

Sometimes people get mixed up when they try to remember which words end in -*ify* and which end in -*efy*. Fortunately, this mixup is easy to sort out.

There are only four common English words that end in -*efy*.

EXAMPLES: liquefy
putrefy
rarefy
stupefy

All the rest end in -*ify*.

EXAMPLES: falsify
rectify
beautify

SPELLCHECK

Determine whether the following words are spelled with -ify *or* -efy.

You must (fortify/fortefy) yourself with hot, nutritious food before a day of skiing.

The (rarefied/rarified) mountain air takes a lot of energy out of you.

The wary babysitter finally decided to (gratefy/gratify) the tireless kids by repeating the joke one last time.

150

89. Memorize the most commonly misspelled words with double consonants

The double letter combinations *cc*, *mm*, *rr*, and *ss* have been previously discussed (see Rules 23, 24, 27, and 28, respectively). Yet how does one recognize which words are spelled with single consonants and which double? Is it *accomodate*, *acomodate*, or *acommodate*? Actually, all three are wrong and if you guessed any of them you shouldn't be *embarrassed*, because you are in the majority. The correct spelling is *accommodate*, with two *c*s and two *m*s. Perhaps the best way to remember this fact is through the memory device (see Rule 100) that the word needs room to *accommodate* the two *c*s and two *m*s.

Other troublesome words that wreak havoc among spellers:

    accessible
    accompany
    accomplishment
    accurate
    accustomed
    commission
    curriculum
    occurrence
    omission
    recommendation

Memorize the spellings of all the above words. If it's easier for you, put to separate memory all of the words that use double letters and all of those that

151

use single. Once you get the hang of it, you'll find that the bad spellings actually appear wrong. On those *occasions*, trust your instincts and sound out the pronunciation. If ever in doubt, consult your dictionary before submitting any copy with questionable spelling.

SPELLCHECK

Choose which spellings are incorrect in the following sentences. If they are wrong, spell them correctly.

Joe was not accesible for the meeting last Thursday regarding the curricculum.

Do not omit the essay question or your reccomendation will be turned down.

The incident occurred three weeks ago.

The major complaint about Bob's spelling is that it lacked accurracy.

Fritz was unaccustommed to criticism.

90. Know when to end words with -ious or -eous

When choosing whether or not to spell a word with either -ious or -eous as the ending, be aware that once again, the English language plays favorites. Most words that end with this sound end in -ious.

EXAMPLES: anxious
cautious
glorious
tedious

Most of the words that end in -eous are technical or scientific words (many of which end in -aceous). Here are the common -eous words.

aqueous
advantageous
beauteous
bounteous
consanguineous
contemporaneous
courageous
courteous
curvaceous
discourteous
erroneous
extraneous
gorgeous

herbaceous
heterogeneous
hideous
homogeneous
instantaneous
miscellaneous
nauseous
outrageous
piteous
righteous
simultaneous
spontaneous
vitreous

SPELLCHECK

List another ten words that end in -ious. If you're feeling industrious, throw in a few that end in -eous that were not on the above list.

91. Know when to end verbs with *-ise* or *-ize*

This is not just a question of American vs. British usage (see Rule 3). In American English, most verbs take *-ize*, but there are some which must take *-ise*.

If the final syllable of the verb is not pronounced as *iz*, it will be written *-ise*.

EXAMPLES: braise   (pronounced *az*)
            raise   (pronounced *az*)
            promise   (pronounced *is*)
            reprise   (pronounced *ez*)

If the *-ise* is part of the root word, instead of being a suffix, the word will be written *-ise*.

EXAMPLES:

advertise	franchise
advise	improvise
apprise	incise
chastise	premise
circumcise	revise
comprise	rise
compromise	surmise
devise	surprise
disguise	televise
excise	

If the ending is being added to a recognizable English word, it should be spelled *-ize*.

EXAMPLES: critic + ize = criticize
           item + ize = itemize
           modern + ize = modernize

SPELLCHECK

Choose the correct spelling in the following sentences.

Sammy does not (despise/despize) Jess, although he should after receiving that brutal insult.

People who (philosophize/philosophise) about utopian societies should think before they speak.

I could use some rigorous (exercize/exercise) after that four-hour film.

Some complications have (arisen/arizen).

Who will (supervize/supervise) the pool deck when the lifeguard takes her lunch hour?

Children and pets respond well to (prayze/praise) and rewards.

92. Know that a few verbs end with -yze, not -ize

Okay, so now you know how to tell when a word is likely to end in either -ise or -ize. Here comes the curve: There are a few verbs that end with -yze. Don't panic, though, as there are not very many:

EXAMPLES: analyze
breathalyze
paralyze
psychoanalyze

Paralyze is really the exception here, since the others are really just variants on *analyze*. *Breathalyze* is a rather ugly new verb, formed from the name of the machine police use to analyze the breath of someone suspected of being drunk (a *breathalyzer*).

The only other thing you need to remember about these words is that in British English, they are always spelled -yse.

SPELLCHECK

Choose the correct spellings in the following sentences. Remember that British spellings are not preferable.

One can (electrolyze/electrolise) unwanted hair.

He is looking into the possibility of purchasing a chain store (franchyze/franchise).

The show "Politically Incorrect" is (satiryzed/satirised/satirized) for your protection.

93. Know what to do with the letter *l*

For some reason, the letter *l* causes a lot more trouble in the English language than most others. The Japanese, of course, are well known to have difficulty pronouncing it, but native English speakers often have just as much trouble knowing what to do with it when it comes to spelling. To make life even more fun, this is one of the areas where American and British usage differ the most (see Rule 3). Here are some rules that should help clear up some of the confusion.

Perhaps the most basic question that arises is, should there be one *l* or two at the end of a word? If the word is only one syllable long and has only one vowel letter, it will probably end in two *l*s. (Words that are based on compounds of these, such as *recall* or *hell-bent*, still follow the rule.) If not, then it ends with one *l*.

EXAMPLES:
bell	appeal
call	initial
fill	soil
mull	trail
toll	wool

EXCEPTIONS:
gal
gel
nil
pal

The big difference between American and British usage comes when it is time to use (or not use) double *l*s. For a full discussion of this, see Rules 67 and 68 on doubling consonants.

Keep in mind that a final double *ll* drops one *l* before the suffix -*ly*; this is easy to remember, because English never allows the same letter to repeat three times in a row. In general, though, the double *ll* remains before suffixes that begin with consonants. (This is true in American English, but not British; the only suffix it is true for in England is -*ness*.)

EXAMPLES: dullness
           enrollment
           skillful
           thralldom
           willful (or *wilful*; both spellings are acceptable)

EXCEPTIONS: fulsome
             the suffix -*t* (smell, spell, spill + t—
             smelt, spelt, spilt)

And finally there are, as always, a few specific words that do their own thing. In this case, the second *l* drops out for no discernible reason.

EXAMPLES: belfry (from bell)
           chilblain (from chill)
           welfare (from well)

SPELLCHECK

Choose the correct spellings in the following sentences.

(Labelling/Labeling) clothes before summer camp is not my favorite pastime.

. The foul (smell/smel) of old cabbage pervaded the O'MacShaugnesseys' house.

I consider Evan a good (pall/pal) of mine.

The shock of hearing the bad news brought a (pall/pal) to his face.

Two (parallel/paralell) lines will never intersect.

94. Know the difference between words ending in *-ous* and *-us*

Another area of confusion arises concerning the difference between words ending in *-ous* or *-us*. Happily, there is an easy rule to remember: Words that end in *-ous* are adjectives, and words that end in *-us* are nouns. The only exceptions are adjectives that are taken directly from the Latin (which used *-us* as an adjectival ending).

ADJECTIVES: dangerous
  desirous
  impetuous
  famous
  spacious

NOUNS: cactus
  impetus
  opus
  virus

EXCEPTIONS: emeritus

SPELLCHECK

Write out six sentences, using the words above correctly.

95. Know which words end in -*cion* and -*cian*

This rule is rather a trick, since there are actually only two common words in the whole English language that end in -*cion*: *coercion* and *suspicion*. However, there are a bunch that end in -*cian*, which creates some difficulties now and then.

As it happens, the words that end in -*cian* are almost all based on words ending in -*ic, -ics*, or -*ical*. Pay special attention to the rule that words ending in -*al*, such as *clinical*, drop those two letters when forming a -*cian* word, such as *clinician*. The majority of -*cian* words describe an individual's job or occupation.

EXAMPLES: magic—magician
music—musician
technical—technician

SPELLCHECK

List as many occupations as you can think of that end in -cian.

96. Know which words end in -*tion*

It is much more complicated to know which words end in -*tion* than in -*cion* (see Rule 95). However, there are some ways to approach the problem.

After a vowel, if the ending of the word is pronounced [shun], it will be written -*tion*.

EXAMPLES: addition
education
position
station

EXCEPTION: There are some words that end in a [shun] sound, but are spelled with a -*ssion* ending. Fortunately, they're a limited group; they're almost always based on words which end in -*ss*, -*mit*, or -*cede*.

EXAMPLES: discuss — discussion
obsess — obsession
procede — procession
transmit — transmission

Words that have any other letters than *l*, *n*, or *r* (see Rule 97) preceding the suffix almost always take -*tion*.

EXAMPLES: action
defection
reception

EXCEPTION: torsion

For words related to or based on words or roots of words which end in *-t* or *-tain*, after the consonants *n* or *r*, the ending is usually spelled *-tion*.

EXAMPLES: abstain—abstention
           assert—assertion
           invent—invention

EXCEPTIONS: attention
             contention
             intention
             mention
             portion
             proportion

SPELLCHECK

Following the above rules, come up with a list of ten more words that end in -tion.

97. Know which words end in -*sion*

The final piece of the -*ion* puzzle involves knowing which words end in -*sion*. Again, there are some rules to help you.

After a vowel, if the ending of the word is pronounced [zhun], it will be written -*sion*.

EXAMPLES: adhesion
decision
persuasion
vision

After the consonant *l*, the ending is written -*sion*.

EXAMPLES: emulsion
expulsion
propulsion

Words that are related to or based on words ending in -*d* or -*se* also take an -*sion* ending.

EXAMPLES: ascend — ascension
comprehend — comprehension
immerse — immersion

EXCEPTIONS: conversion
diversion
extroversion
introversion
aspersion
dimension
excursion

incursion
mansion
pension
recursion
scansion
tension
version

SPELLCHECK

Using all the rules you know, come up with at least fifteen words that end with either -sion or -tion.

98. Remember to use apostrophes correctly

Apostrophes are the little punctuation marks that are used to indicate contractions and possession: They look like this ('). Generally, of course, their use is discussed in grammar and punctuation books. However, misuse of apostrophes can create spelling mistakes, so they deserve some mention here as well.

One common source of error is how to use apostrophes after abbreviations. The rule is that abbreviations followed by periods take apostrophes, but others do not. A store offering a sale on "CD's" should cut not only their prices but also that incorrect apostrophe. On the other hand, if a Ph.D. candidate wants to talk about her dissertation, she needs that apostrophe, since it is a *Ph.D.'s* thesis.

There are some apostrophe rules to keep in mind when spelling words that indicate possession. Possessives are nouns that indicate ownership. To form the possessive of a singular noun, add *'s*. This holds true even if the word already ends with *s*.

EXAMPLES: Charles**'s** hat
horse**'s** tail
record**'s** jacket

Apostrophes for surnames can be confusing, especially when referring to a possessive plural. If one is referring to a husband and wife who have a shared surname ending in *s*, it's typical to add an *-es'* to let the reader know that both individuals are included in the possession.

EXAMPLES: Herb Smith — Mr. Smith's dog
           Herb and Myrtle Smith — the Smiths'
               dog
           Sigmund and Tuttle Williams — the Wil-
               liamses' cat

Possessives for plural words are formed by adding
only the apostrophe.

EXAMPLES: two clubs' joint meeting place
           students' study area
           books' covers

Finally, apostrophes are also used to indicate
omission. Contracted words always require an apostrophe to show that letters have been left out.

EXAMPLES: don't (represents the omitted *o*)
           y'all (represents the omitted *ou*)
           can't (represents the omitted *no*)
           she'll (represents the omitted *wi*)

SPELLCHECK

*Decide whether to insert an apostrophe in the itali-
cized words.*

What will the *Smiths* remember most about the
1990s?

The *grasss* color should be green, but ever since the
kids pool was built, it has been brown.

Chris will file for *workers* compensation to pay for
his hospital *bills*.

Wont you accompany me to the *movies* this evening?

Eileens parents are taking her to see a show.

99. Remember what *etc.* stands for and how to spell it

Another example of the mischief abbreviations can make in spelling comes with the term *etc.* It is commonly used, but many people forget (or fail to realize altogether) that it is an abbreviation of the Latin phrase *et cetera*, meaning "and other things." Forgetting where it comes from, people have found some creative new spellings for the term. Stick with the correct one.

Since English has, to a certain extent, taken over the word, there is also now an acceptable English plural form: *etceteras*. This is used (occasionally) to refer to a miscellany of odds and ends. The standard abbreviation *etc.* should generally be kept only in fairly casual writing.

100. When all else fails, use memory devices

If you find that rote memorization is not always a reliable way to remember tricky spellings, try memory devices. Come up with phrases or ideas that you can associate with the spelling of particular words. Also known as mnemonic devices, these memory aids work best if you make them up yourself. The most popular spelling device is the adage "*I* before *E* Except after *C*, Or when sounded like *ay* As in *neighbor* or *weigh*," which is helpful for spelling many words such as *friend* and *receive*.

Here are some more memory devices that you may want to remember.

EXAMPLES: *Weird* is spelled weirdly, an exception to the "I before E" rule.

A *secretary* can keep your secrets. (This will prevent you from spelling it "secra-tary.")

A *principal* is a person who is your pal. (This will help avoid confusion with "principle," meaning doctrine.)

A *knowledgeable* person remembers the silent *e*.

Your *mission* is not to forget the second *s* in *omission*.

The *cemetery* gravestones are full of *cement*.

Though you shouldn't spend time making elaborate memory devices that may be harder to remember than the spellings themselves, creating and using your own word associations can be a useful and fun way to help you spell troublesome words.

SPELLCHECK

Create memory devices for the following words. (If you already know how to spell these words, make a list of four others that continuously stump you.) Tomorrow, ask yourself if you remember both the devices you created and the proper spellings of these words. If not, try again.

    carousel
    governor
    parallel
    manageable

101. DON'T TRUST YOUR SPELL-CHECKER!

Why should anyone bother to learn how to spell anymore, when it seems that computers all have spell-check programs? Because no matter how weak a speller you are, and no matter how powerful your computer is, you are still a million times smarter than any spell-check program yet available.

Computers seem smart, because they can do certain operations with incredible speed. But, all they're really doing is following the instructions they are given, no more. There isn't a spell-check program available today smart enough to recognize the error in this sentence:

BAD: "I just came form the dentist."

Why not? Because *form* is a legitimate English word. Unfortunately, in the above example, it is a typo for the word *from*. A human proofreader would catch this, because he or she would read the sentence and see at once that, in context, this is not the right word. This is the sort of thing many spelling mistakes come down to, and in such cases spell checkers are of no help. If your error creates an unrecognizable pattern, then the spell-checker will catch it, but otherwise it may not.

Alternatively, if an error is serious enough, the spell-checker may suggest a completely different word than the one you want. If you are depending on it too heavily, you may have no way to find the correct spelling of the word you do want.

Moreover, you have to keep in mind that not all

spell-checkers are created equal. If you are used to relying on a full-scale, customized dictionary as part of your spell-check program, you will be in for a rude shock the first time you use another system that isn't as sophisticated as yours.

This doesn't mean you shouldn't use your spell-checker at all. On the contrary, it can be very helpful in catching typos and some misspellings. Just don't think that they can take the place of your own knowledge. In the end, your judgment and ability to reason will prevail over the technical capability of any machine.

The 101 Quiz

Congratulations! If you have read this entire book and think you know the most important 101 spelling rules, test yourself by taking this quiz.

There are at least 101 spelling mistakes in the following paragraphs. Find as many of them as you can.

Once apon a time, there was a briliant student named Lloyd hoose only problem was spelling. Aside from the orrendous mistakes he made every thyme he rote anything, he was one of the clevverest boyz at Dikkshionery High Skool. His score on the Essay-T astoundded all of his teachers and empressed all of his freinds and akwaintances. Beeing a preminent sceintist, computer analist, hisstorian, and enjineer, responsible for inventing a programe called the "Majjical Grammer Chekker" for use on all tipes of computers, and for reserrching Volume 101 of *The Ensyclopeadia of Western Hisstory* by the age of aiteen, Loid loveed to learn and thingk. He was voted "Most Likkly to Suckseed" at gradiation. Summhow, he had alweys covered up his spellling deffishency by exselling in other arias.

To proove his inteligence to himselph and uthers, Loids' lifelong dreem was too win the Spelling B helled anualy in his town, skedjuled for the day befour his gradiation. Loid fellt that if he rangked iether first or secont place amung all of the other stoodents at Dikkshionerry High, he wood undispyootedly be the smartest gye in the cownty and graduait proudder then ever. Tharefour, a fyoo munths befoar the big day, he set out to learn all of the spelling rooles he could possibley learn. Nobuddy has ever sean such detirmination.

174

But dais, weaks, munths past, and still Loid had nought eaven masterred the spelling of his own name (spelled on his berth certiphicate *Lloyd*). As it hapens, his parrents had taut Loid to spell foneti-cally as an infint. This meens thet he cud spell wurds as he thout thay shoud look, but not with enny re-gard to the rooles of Inglisch spelling. Not noeing rools maykes it hard to remember eckseptions. Loid was never abel to spell anything coreccly becozz he just could'nt stop spelling his wurds fonetically. Neadless to say, he was the first one iliminated at the anual Spelling B that yeer.

Even tho he had been a prodiggy as a child, excel-ing in all other subgects, this spelling problem had detered him from fulfiling his dreem of winning the Spelling B, thereby rendering pore Loid a faileur in his oan mind. (Note: Loid di'dnt have acksess to *Spelling 101*. This hapened a long tyme agoe.)

The morral of this story is: *Read, Study, and Re-member the Rules Outlined in this Book*, if you want to become the best writter and communnicater that you can B!

Answer Key to The 101 Quiz

Once upon a time, there was a brilliant student named Lloyd, whose only problem was spelling. Aside from the horrendous mistakes he made every time he wrote anything, he was one of the cleverest boys at Dictionary High School. His score on the SAT astounded all of his teachers and impressed all of his friends and acquaintances. Being a preeminent scientist, computer analyst, historian, and engineer— responsible for inventing a program called the "Magical Grammar Checker" for use on all types of computers, and for researching Volume 101 of *The Encyclopedia of Western History* by the age of eighteen—Lloyd loved to learn and think. He was voted "Most Likely to Succeed" at graduation. Somehow, he had always covered up his spelling deficiency by excelling in other areas.

To prove his intelligence to himself and others, Lloyd's lifelong dream was to win the Spelling Bee held annually in his town, scheduled for the day before graduation. Lloyd felt that if he ranked either first or second place among all of the other students at Dictionary High, he would undisputedly be the smartest guy in the county and graduate prouder than ever. Therefore, a few months before the big day, he set out to learn all of the spelling rules he could possibly learn. Nobody has ever seen such determination.

But days, weeks, months passed, and still Lloyd had not even mastered the spelling of his own name (spelled on his birth certificate *Lloyd*). As it happens, his parents had taught Lloyd to spell phonetically as an infant. This means he could spell words as he thought they should look, but not with any regard to the rules of English spelling. Not knowing rules makes it hard to remember exceptions. Lloyd was never able to spell anything correctly because he just couldn't stop spelling his words phonetically. Needless to say, he was the first one eliminated at the Spelling Bee that year.

Even though he had been a prodigy as a child, excelling in all other subjects, this spelling problem had deterred him from fulfilling his dream of winning the Spelling Bee, thereby rendering poor Lloyd a failure in his own mind. (Note: Lloyd didn't have access to *Spelling 101*. This happened a long time ago.)

The moral of this story is: *Read, Study, and Remember the Rules Outlined in this Book*, if you want to become the best writer and communicator that you can be!